		Book of Runes	Healing Runes	Relationship Runes	Germanic Name
1	ᛗ	The Self	Innocence	Loving Kindness	*Mannaz*
2	ᚷ	Partnership	Trust	Commitment	*Gebo*
3	ᚨ	Signals	Guilt	Communication	*Ansuz*
4	ᛟ	Separation	Grief	Home & Family	*Othila*
5	ᚢ	Strength	Gratitude	Support	*Uruz*
6	ᛈ	Initiation	Love	Intimacy	*Perth*
7	ᚾ	Constraint	Shame	Limitations	*Nauthiz*
8	ᛝ	Fertility	Faith	Renewal	*Inguz*
9	ᛇ	Defence	Denial	Respect	*Eihwaz*
10	ᛉ	Protection	Boundaries	Mutual Trust	*Algiz*
11	ᚠ	Possessions	Honesty	Abundance	*Fehu*
12	ᚹ	Joy	Serenity	Celebration	*Wunjo*
13	ᛃ	Harvest	Patience	Perseverance	*Jera*
14	ᚲ	Opening	Acceptance	Inner Peace	*Kano*
15	ᛏ	Warrior	Courage	Passion	*Teiwaz*
16	ᛒ	Growth	Prayer	Right Action	*Berkana*
17	ᛗ	Movement	Forgiveness	Letting Go	*Ehwaz*
18	ᛚ	Flow	Humor	Change	*Laguz*
19	ᚻ	Disruption	Anger	Challenges	*Hagalaz*
20	ᚱ	Journey	Surrender	Harmony	*Raido*
21	ᚦ	Gateway	Wisdom	Compromise	*Thurisaz*
22	ᛞ	Breakthrough	Hope	Purpose	*Dagaz*
23	ᛁ	Standstill	Fear		
24	ᛊ	Wholeness	Compassio		
25	☐	Unknowable	The Divine		

GW00778379

RELATIONSHIP
RUNES

Also by Ralph Blum

The Book of Runes

RunePlay

RuneCards

Healing Runes
(with Susan Loughan)

The Serenity Runes
(with Susan Loughan and Bronwyn Jones)

Also by Bronwyn Jones

The Serenity Runes
(with Ralph Blum and Susan Loughan)

RELATIONSHIP RUNES

A Compass for the Heart

Commentary by
Ralph Blum *and* Bronwyn Jones

THOMAS DUNNE BOOKS
St. Martin's Press ⚏ New York

THOMAS DUNNE BOOKS
An imprint of St. Martin's Press

Illustrations: compass and lotus by Anthony Duke;
keys and sword by Jancis Salerno

ISBN 0-312-32098-1

First U.S. Edition

1 3 5 7 9 10 8 6 4 2

AN EDDISON•SADD EDITION
Edited, designed and produced by
Eddison Sadd Editions Limited
St Chad's House, 148 King's Cross Road
London WC1X 9DH

Phototypeset in Palatino and Calligraphic 421
using QuarkXPress on Apple Macintosh
Printed and produced by Hung Hing Printing Co., China

Dedication

CONTENTS

Before you read any further and discover how others have used the Runes, we invite you to pick your first Relationship Rune and experience directly the ways of this ancient and contemporary Oracle. So take a moment to relax and let go of all the cares and worries of your day. Then ask: *What do I need to know for my life right now?*

Reach into your bag, draw out a single stone, and find its match among the twenty-five Runes pictured on the inside front cover of your book. Next, turn to the page number given beneath that Rune and read the Interpretation, paying particular attention to those phrases that hold special meaning for you.

Drawing this Rune marks the first step of a journey. Acknowledge this new beginning by inscribing your Rune in the blank stone provided below, along with its name, this day's date, the location you are in, and a few words that convey some aspect of the Interpretation that you find relevant to your life.

Name of the Relationship Rune

Date:
Location:
Aspect:

It is our prayer that these Runes will guide and serve you well on all journeys of the heart. And to that end, we offer an old Norse blessing: *Verthi ther ath gothi...* "May the good come to you." May it indeed.

Invocation

We do not know your holy name, we only know
You are the One from whom all blessings flow.
So it is right and good and only fitting
That we stand before you now in listening
    and in prayer,
Only proper that we rehearse your Presence
Every step of our days together,
Each moment on our journey home,
This journey, so magnificent when
    our wills and thine align.
O You whose ways are our ways when
    we let them be,
Hear our prayer.

> *Provide us with a set of sacred tools,*
> *Whose right use can be lovingly detected in each other's eyes;*
> *Tools that loose their benediction on our ancient bondage*
> *And heal us from all wounds of separation;*
> *Tools that, in our hands, define us as your children.*
> *And so we offer up the fruit of this our prayer.*
> *Help us, we pray, to bring it forth*
> *From the highest possible place*
> *And for the greatest possible good.*

Amen

Preface

When Ralph Blum and Bronwyn Jones phoned me one morning and asked if I would write an introduction to their new book, *Relationship Runes: A Compass for the Heart,* I was delighted. I have known Ralph for over twenty years, and his work with the Runes has been an inspiration to me, as well as a gift to many others. Turning the light of the Runes onto the sometimes dark tangles of our relationships seemed to me a perfect use for this ancient oracular system.

The manuscript arrived shortly thereafter, followed by another phone call. "Before you start," Ralph said, "draw a Rune. Let that Rune guide you as you write." I took his advice. The Rune I drew was number 25 ⬜, the Blank Rune, symbolizing the Mystery, the Unknowable, the Divine.

I can think of no more suitable Rune to inspire this introduction. All relationships are a step into the unknown. The greatest gift a relationship may offer us is mystery, the opportunity for discovery and for learning something new about ourselves and about our friend or beloved. And just as the physicists say that the universe emerges from quantum relationships, so at the heart of every relationship lies the spirit of that emergence, the spirit of the sacred. When we enter into a loving relationship, we are replicating in our own unique way the primal act that gives birth to creation.

What struck me most about the Rune I drew was its appearance. It is blank, an open space. The Rune is literally a clean slate, unmarked on either side.

To me this open space is the greatest gift a relationship can offer. As I said in a book of my own, *Blessing: The Art and the Practice*, to surround others in our thoughts and spirit with open space—a clear space within which they can find the room to be purely themselves and answer the call of their own unique spirits—is one of the greatest blessings we can offer. In a world in which so much conspires to tell us what to do, who to be, how to look, how to behave, the gift of being allowed to discover and be ourselves is precious. It is a gift that often can only be offered with love, for usually only love can find the trust in another and the joy on his or her behalf to make that gift.

To bless another with the gift of open space means giving up our projections upon him or her; it means foregoing attempts at control or manipulation. It means a willingness to let him be himself or her be herself, and to love that person just as much for the differences between you as for the similarities. It means to recognize and honor the unique expression of divinity within that person. It means to accept him or her as a mystery that cannot be wholly known, wholly understood, or wholly familiar.

This is not easy. Relationships develop histories in the same way that comets develop tails as they plunge towards the sun: long trails of memories, of old pleasures and old hurts, of negotiations and compromises, of habits and familiarities. And just as we recognize a comet in the sky because it has a tail, so we often recognize relationships by their histories. We wake up in the morning and we do not see a person next to us in bed or across the breakfast table or getting ready for work; we see a wife or husband, a role, a familiar shape, a remembered argument, a remembered embrace. We see them and we see all the yesterdays we have spent together. We see them and we see all the hopes we may once have had, the dreams deferred or lost.

But if I see you in your mystery, in your divinity, with the power of the open space and the Blank Rune, then I see that, like creation itself, you are being recreated every day, even every moment. And that recreation is possible for me as well.

My wife and I have been married twenty-one years, which is long for some in my generation but hardly worth mentioning to many folks in my father's generation for whom marriages and relationships have lasted well over sixty or seventy years. My parents had been married sixty-four years when my mother died. During that time one accumulates a lot of memories. But for Dad, each day with Mom was like the first day they were married, and that is how it is for my wife and me.

This takes attention. It is easy to fall into history. It's always around us, always trailing after us catching the light of our attention. But all it takes is a mental shift, a willingness to see the other as if for the first time, to push past the inertia of memory and see the mystery, the unknowableness, the divine in one's partner and in one's self. I rejoice in the familiarity of my wife and the memory of twenty-one very good years. But each day I rejoice even more in looking for what I have yet to discover in her, for the person who has yet to reveal herself, for the one who will step out from mystery that day and present herself to the world. I have yet to be disappointed, and as long as I follow the promise of the Blank Rune, I never will be.

I think that for God, each day is like the first day. As the old hymn says, "Morning has broken like the first morning." That is the power of the Blank Rune. That is the power of relationship, to learn enough about another, to realize we will never know all there is to know about that other. It is to love another enough to liberate him or her from our projections and expectations, giving that person open space within which to be themselves. That is the blessing of relationship. In a world that always seeks to press us into one mould or another, where else should we feel free to be ourselves, to dream our dreams, to explore the mystery at the core of our own hearts, and to touch the sacredness within us, except in the presence of one who loves us. Where else but in relationship?

That relationships so often fail to find this open space, so often neglect to keep burning the fire of each other's divinity and newness, is a tragedy. It happens when relationships get lost in the tangle of memories, of hurts real or imagined, of dreams forgotten or abandoned. It happens when relationships become robotic, automatic, and reflexive, one knee jerk triggering another. It happens when we forget that we have a power to bless each other and to be blessed and that blessing is the secret heart of relationship.

How wonderful, then, for Ralph and Bronwyn to reach into an ancient system and come up with a compass for our hearts. There is wisdom and love in this book; its pages have been immersed in it. And there is the knowledge and wisdom of the Runes themselves, each one a possible doorway into ourselves, into each other, and into mystery, wonder, and the blessing of relationship.

I commend this book to you most willingly and happily. May each of the Runes be a blessing to you in your relationship. In particular, whether you draw it or not, may the Blank Rune of the Divine and of the Mystery be the foundation and the arch of all you are together.

David Spangler
Philosopher, Writer, Teacher

Blessings

It is impossible to bless and to judge at the same time. So hold constantly as a deep, hallowed, intoned thought that desire to bless, for truly then shall you become a peacemaker, and one day you shall, everywhere, behold the very face of God.
— Pierre Pradervand, *The Gentle Art of Blessing*

Surely a blessing is also a flow of life force between ourselves and others or between ourselves and the sacred. It's an act of connection. It restores through love a circulation of spirit among us that may have become blocked, forgotten or overlooked. A blessing reconnects us to the community of creation.
— David Spangler, *Blessing: The Art and the Practice*

INTRODUCTION

The brightest light is love. The lamps will change
but the light is still the same.

—Neil "Poppy" Letterman

We need a world safe for differences.

—Alan W. Slifka

Recently we found a quote in which Deepak Chopra praised Carlos Castaneda for "paving the way for the future evolution of human consciousness." *Paving the way*—a labourer's image evoking the mason's craft and building on the square. A good way to put it. What a relief from the white water of swift innovation, shooting rapids after rapids in the electronic millrace of the dot.com revolution.

With technologies and tools outdated almost as quickly as they come to market, it is reassuring to be reminded by a voice we trust that the expansion and growth of human consciousness is still attained by treading the cobblestones of ideas, insights and revelations, one stone, one step, one decision at a time. At such a benign pace, the danger of being left behind is slender-to-none. In fact, there is an oracular principle that affirms: *In the life of the Spirit we are always at the beginning.*

Creating this compass for the conduct of meaningful relationships has been a considerable challenge, one that has required us to confront our own issues time and time again. Every pernicious form of negative behaviour—anger, impatience,

17

resentment, lack of trust, the need to be right—came up for review, creating havoc in our daily work and in our emotions. And as each issue presented itself, whether explosively or subtly, we found it impossible to move forward with the writing until we were willing to communicate more honestly and learned to work together in new ways.

We discovered the wisdom of taking a break from each other and from the work. And on those unfortunate occasions when both our needles got stuck in the red, we sometimes found it wise to stay apart for an entire day. Eventually, we learned to treat what was happening between us with curiosity and even with kindness. In our worst moments, we still made the effort to find our way back from anger to laughter. Over time the many shifts that occurred between us allowed the Oracle to align with its own true North. To become, in fact, a well-calibrated compass for the heart.

The primary purpose of *Relationship Runes: A Compass for the Heart* is to assist you in meeting both the challenges that arise with an intimate partner and the issues that come up between close friends, family members, co-workers and people who relate through a community of interest or come together in faith-based fellowships. In effect, this oracular instrument is intended to support meaningful relationships of every kind, beginning and ending with your relationship with yourself and the Divine.

We trust you will find, as we have, that this mysterious process—identifying your issue, picking a Rune, then watching for the words that speak to you as you read the Interpretation— will serve as a guide to right action in your life. Ultimately, it is the interactive nature of the Runes that is compelling. For as you engage with the Oracle, rather than asking an outside authority to tell you what to do, you are choosing to listen to the wisdom of your own inner knowing.

May the Runes assist you in getting your bearings in all weathers, and in making the necessary course adjustments on the journey of loving relationship.

Ralph Blum and Bronwyn Jones
March 2003
Idyllwild, California

Concerning Love and Friendship

For the first time I know what love is; what friends are… Love is seeking for a way of life; the way that cannot be followed alone; the resonance of all spiritual and physical things… Friendship is another form of love—more passive perhaps, but full of the transmitting and acceptance of things like thunderclouds and grass and the clean granite of reality.

—Ansel Adams, photographer,
in a letter to Cedric Wright, 10 June 1937

I

RENDEZVOUS AT REDHILL

The philosophy of waiting is sustained by
all the oracles of the universe.

—Ralph Waldo Emerson

I'm convinced that life is 10 per cent what happens to me, and
90 per cent how I react to it. We are in charge of our attitude.
—Rev. Charles Swindoll

On an early spring afternoon in 1977, I found myself in the English countryside standing in the rain outside a dreary, semi-detached house in the town of Redhill, Surrey. I had come there at the suggestion of an old friend who told me, "There's someone you ought to meet." When I asked why, he said, "Go meet her, you'll see."

I rang the bell and was ushered in by a handsome, auburn-haired woman who sat me down across a table from her. Between us lay a jumble of small clay tiles.

"What are those?" I asked.

"Those are Runes," she replied.

"I beg your pardon?"

"Runes."

I had heard of Runes and vaguely remembered them from Tolkein's *The Fellowship of the Ring,* and so I said, "Ah, yes, Runes. I suppose they tell you the future?"

"No, they tell you *the present.*"

Time seemed to slow down as she laid out the Runes and then interpreted them for me. I remember the clicking of those glazed clay tablets, no larger than a thumbnail and the colour of dry earth. I remember rain sweeping the rooftop and slapping on the windowpanes. As to the content of the Rune reading, I remember nothing. When she had finished and asked me if I had any questions, I said, "Where can I buy a set of those stones?"

"There's a woman on Trindles Road who bakes them in her oven. They will cost you ten pounds."

I ordered a set and eventually my bag of Runes arrived along with several Xeroxed sheets that provided a brief Interpretation for each Rune. I played with them a few times, then forgot about them until one evening several months later.

I was back on my farm in New Milford, Connecticut. My life was in total disarray. I was broke, depressed, out of work, my wife had just left me, I couldn't sleep, and I was dusting books in the library, when the bag of Runes fell off the shelf into my hand.

Standing there in the half-dark, with the tree frogs croaking out their night song, I heard myself saying out loud to the stones,

"Alright, time to get serious—I need to know what order you come in."

But there was a problem: the Xeroxed pages that accompanied the stones were not numbered, so I didn't know which page of Runes followed which. Although I might have waited until morning, then gone to the library to learn the true order of this ancient Germanic-Norse alphabet, fortunately the idea never occurred to me. As a result, since that summer evening, my life has been shaped by a trip to the library not taken.

I sat at my desk and spread the Runes out, face down. Mixing them around, so I wouldn't know one from another, I said a prayer, asking that my connection with this Oracle be held in the Light and be of service to the greatest good.

Then, one by one, I turned over the 25 stones and set them out in five rows, allowing an alphabet that had a perfectly good 2000-year-old order to rearrange itself.

Already I had noticed that there was something unorthodox about this alphabet. The original Germanic "Futhark" alphabet—so-called because its first six letters were f, u, th, a, r and k—contained 24 letters, each bearing its own symbol or glyph. The twenty-fifth Rune in my set was blank. It was what philologists would call a "later intrusion," having entered the alphabet sometime between A.D. 200 and 1977. It occurred to me that this Blank Rune might stand for the presence of the Divine in all transactions. Some months later, when I showed the first draft of The Book of Runes to anthropologist Margaret Mead, she said, "Remarkable—an alphabet that goes A, B, C, D… X, Y, God."

Here's how the Runes ordered themselves on that summer night:

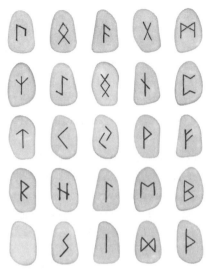

What immediately caught my attention was the fact that the Blank Rune had placed itself in the left-hand corner of the bottom row. And yet, if it represented the Unknowable, and was in fact the "God-Rune," why wasn't it in last place, on the right side? Then I recalled reading somewhere that Runes, like certain other ancient alphabets, could be read from right to left. That would give the Blank Rune its pre-eminent place.

Then I glanced up at the right-hand corner, top row, and there was M the Rune called *Mannaz* which, according to my Xeroxed pages, stood for "Man, Woman, the Self." At that moment I sensed for the first time that I was in the presence of a mystery. *Here was an alphabet that begins with the self and ends with the*

Divine, a map for the journey of the self returning to its Source.

I picked up the Rune of *The Self*, ᛗ, and sat quietly, breathing in the summer night and listening to the tree frogs, until these words came to me and I began to write:

> *The starting point is the self. Its essence is water. Only clarity, willingness to change, is effective now. A correct relationship to your self is primary, for from it flow all possible correct relationships with others and with the Divine...*

When I finished writing down my thoughts about The Self, I moved on to the next Rune, and the next. Whenever the flow dried up, I would turn to the *I Ching*—the ancient Chinese *Book of Changes*, an Oracle dear to the sage Confucius—and ask for a commentary on the Rune in question. And so I continued through the night, taking my cues from the Xeroxed pages, recording my thoughts, and being assisted when stuck by "oracular cross-talk," one oracle revealing the wisdom of the other.

Almost before I noticed, it was dawn. Everything was wonderfully still. I held the twenty-fifth Rune, *The Blank Rune*, in my hand and began to write:

> *Blank is the end, blank the beginning—this is the Rune of total trust and should be taken as exciting evidence of your most immediate contact with your own true destiny which, time and again, rises like the phoenix from the ashes of what we call fate.*

This sentence struck me as curious for several reasons. First of all, I don't usually write sentences of that complexity and length.

Neither the phrasing nor the style was familiar to me. Then too, the words "fate" and "destiny," which I tend to use more or less interchangeably, seemed to be established in a formal relationship to one another. As if to say, you must burn your fate like fuel in order to achieve your destiny.

When I completed my notes for the final Rune, the sun was coming up, its rays breaking through the leaves of the ginkgo tree outside my window. I opened the calendar to note the time and date. It was the morning of 22nd June. I had written through the night of the summer solstice. Allowing those Xeroxed pages to serve as guides for my meditations, I had heard the wise voice of the Oracle.

The promise found in the final words of the twenty-fifth Rune is most encouraging: "Whenever you draw the *Blank Rune*, take heart: know that the work of self-change is progressing in your life." Looking back over the decades that separate me from that far-off June night, I realize how much has changed in my understanding of myself and in my connection with the Divine. The Oracle continues to be a strong teacher, helping me to stay present, to live my life in trust, and to navigate by my own inner guidance.

And so the journey that began on a rainy afternoon in Redhill, continues with this Interpretation of the Runes, this compass for the conduct of meaningful relationships, this compass for the heart.

—R.B.

Transforming inner negativity,

repairing the damage of destructive emotion,

transmitting the blessings of the enlightened,

compassionate heart and awakened mind—

this skilful means of wisdom in action

becomes medicine for the mind

and a shield for the heart.

—Tarthang Tulku,
A Mandala of Protection

In Praise of Oracles

oracle 1. *among the ancient Greeks and Romans, a) the place where, or medium by which, deities were consulted; b) the revelation or response of a medium or priest; 2. a) any person or agency believed to be in communication with a deity; b) any person of great knowledge or wisdom; c) opinions or statements of any such oracle; 3. the holy of holies of the ancient Jewish Temple.*
　　　　　　　　　　　　—Webster's New World Dictionary

Function determines form, use confers meaning, and an Oracle always responds to the requirements of the time in which it is consulted, and to the needs of those consulting it.
　　　　　　　　　　　　—The Book of Runes

There is hardly a culture that has not, at some time in its history, supported and honored an oracular tradition, a technique for entering into communication with the Divine. Pre-Christian Greece was known for its thriving centres of oracular activity, the most notable of which were located at Delphi,

Ephesus and Dodona. The Romans studied the flight of birds, the arrangement of clouds, and patterns formed on water, while in Africa shamans heated stones in a fire and then interpreted the cracks that appeared as they cooled. The Germanic and Norse peoples notched symbols on pieces of wood that they then read to learn the will of their gods. The Chinese still consult the 4,000-year-old *I Ching*, or *Book of Changes*, considered by many people around the world as a wise source of possibilities and options. To this day, even in exile, the Tibetan people have a State Oracle, a priest who travels in the entourage of the Dalai Lama.

The Judeo-Christian tradition is richly informed by the oracular as well. Do you remember the Voice in the whirlwind or the burning bush from which God spoke to Moses? Most intriguing of all the Old Testament Oracles were the *Urim* and *Thummin*, gemstones worn on the breastplates of the priests and used by them to learn Jehovah's will in difficult situations. The Annunciation by the Archangel Gabriel, when he brought the good news to Mary, was an oracular event, as was the selection by lots of a new apostle to take the place of Judas Iscariot.

In the nineteenth and early twentieth centuries, many people in the United States opened their Bibles at random when they needed counsel, pointed to a passage and read the words that lay beneath their fingers. Some people still start each day in that way. Similar use was made of the dictionary which, by the 1880s, was commonly known as "Noah Webster's Oracle."

The Runes as an Oracular System

The first alphabetic script for the purpose of writing was introduced to the Germanic tribes of Europe by Etruscan traders more than

2,000 years ago. From earliest recorded times, the glyphs or letters of this Germanic alphabet were known as *runen*: "a secret thing, a mystery." The use of symbols or signs (each of which possessed a specific meaning and a unique sound) to convey words or thoughts, was looked upon by pre-literate people as nothing less than magical.

Carved onto twigs and bones, painted or incised on stones, these 24 runic symbols, among the precursors to our modern Western alphabet, were used by tribal leaders to learn the will of the gods for the people. The earliest recorded description of this practice comes from the Roman historian Tacitus Germanicus and dates from around A.D. 98:

> *They cut a branch from a fruit-bearing tree and divide it into pieces which they mark with certain distinctive signs (notae) and scatter at random onto a white cloth. Then, the priest of the community, if the lots are consulted publicly, or the father of the family, if it is done privately, after invoking the gods and with eyes raised to heaven, picks up three pieces, one at a time, and interprets them according to the signs previously marked upon them.*

It is with these 24 original runic symbols—plus the *Blank Rune*, a later intrusion representing the Divine—that we are concerned in the *Relationship Runes: A Compass for the Heart.*

Oracular traditions are as diverse as the cultures that nurture and are served by them. In addressing the Runes as a contemporary Oracle, you are aligning yourself with one of the most ancient and sacred traditions known to humankind. It is our pleasure, then, to present you with a compass whose coordinates are twenty-five of the fundamental aspects of a loving relationship.

Security in a relationship lies neither in looking back to what it was in nostalgia, nor forward to what it might be in dread or anticipation, but living in the present relationship and accepting it as it is now. For relationships, too, must be like islands. One must accept them for what they are here and now, within our limits— islands, surrounded and interrupted by the sea, continually visited and abandoned by the tides.

—Anne Morrow Lindbergh, *A Gift From the Sea*

— 3 —
SACRED LISTENING

If anyone speaks, let him speak as the oracles of God.
—1 Peter 4:11

You could say the Runes are just another way of calling home.
—Father Bede Griffiths

Have you ever found the solution to a problem in the words of a popular song playing on the radio? Hearing from the Divine can be as simple and immediate as a rainstorm that bursts from the skies at the very moment you are praying for your troubles to be washed away. The Divine addresses each of us in a language we can understand, speaking with impeccable timing and perfect pitch, sometimes with the force of a whirlwind, and at others with great delicacy of wit and subtle humor.

One evening, during a late-night television interview, host Charlie Rose asked Sister Wendy, the art historian nun, how she spent a typical day. When she answered that she began by praying for four or five hours, Rose wanted to know what she found to ask for that took so long. Sister Wendy replied,

"Oh, Charlie, I don't *ask* for anything. I *listen*."

Some years ago, the late Benedictine monk, Father Bede Griffiths, described the Runes as "another way of calling home." He spoke of "sacred listening" as common both to prayer and to the oracular. A case could be made, he said, for the oracular nature of prayer itself. For whenever we say, "my prayers have been answered," we are partaking of the oracular tradition. And doing so by a special kind of listening.

Oracles in general, and the Runes in particular, are for the use of all who welcome the Divine into their lives. The Divine speaks, and when we hear, that is an oracular moment. If, however, you find yourself wondering how to tell true messages from the false ones, start by considering the nature and quality of the information received. Then ask three simple questions: *Does this message foster healing? Does it promote unity? Does it encourage love?* These same criteria apply whenever you consult the Runes.

When to Consult the Runes

In every meaningful relationship, there will be times when it is helpful to have the support of a wise friend, someone who can see the issue clearly and offer fair comment. In our experience, the Runes are just such a friend.

Over the years, many readers have shared with us stories of how "playing with the Runes" led to profound insights and breakthroughs in their lives. The Runes can prove most useful when you have too little reliable information to make an informed decision, and yet a decision is called for. However, since the purpose of the Runes is to serve as a guide to right action, it is the nature of the Oracle not to provide answers but rather *to point you in the direction where you can discover the answer for yourself.*

One basic rule that governs the use of an oracular instrument is this: *be present.* And since the future emerges from the actions we take in the present, *the present moment is the only place where change can happen.* After all, when have you ever managed to make a mistake in the future?

When some situation in your life is causing you confusion or pain, rather than asking a "yes/no" question, frame the problem as an issue: *The issue is my relationship... The issue is my work...* Then draw a Rune from your bag. As you read the Interpretation, pay attention to any phrase or sentence that strikes a chord with you. This simple recognition will often bring about a shift, an effortless transition from confusion to clarity, from self-doubt to a peaceful mind.

In time, we hope you too will come to share our deep appreciation for the Runes as a trustworthy and useful friend. And yet whatever the Runes may be—from a well-calibrated compass for conduct to a bridge between the self and the Divine—the energy that engages them is your own and, ultimately, the wisdom as well.

The term "conscious relationship" refers to the concept of engaging in a one-on-one intimate alliance in which two people clearly make it their intention to deal with all the challenges, expectations, projections, cultural myths, and habitual behaviour inherently involved in a relationship of this nature.

The commitment is to maintain the integrity of the individual while surrendering to the requirements of the partnership.

—Cathleen Rountree, *The Heart of Marriage*

CONSULTING THE RUNES ORACLE

Oracles do not absolve you of the responsibility for selecting your future, but rather direct your attention towards those inner choices that may be the most important elements in determining that future.

—Dr. Martin D. Rayner

The desire and pursuit of the whole is called love.

—Plato

Since meaningful relationships often provide us with our most significant challenges as well as our best opportunities for growth, *Relationship Runes: A Compass for the Heart* is offered as an interactive guide to help you make your way on the lifelong journey of relationship. It is our hope that this book, together with its bag of 25 marked stones, will serve as a compass for conduct and a guide to right action, both in your personal relationships and in the world.

Whenever you consult the Runes, it is important to remember that an Oracle is not meant to predict the future or to give you specific answers. Instead the Runes you draw will point you in the direction where you will discover the answers for yourself.

CONSULTING THE RUNES

If you are a newcomer to the Runes, it can be helpful to draw a Rune each morning, record it in a notebook and let it serve as your *Rune of Right Action* for the day. Say you draw *Eihwaz*, ⟨⟩, the Rune of Respect, when things are a bit strained between you and your partner. You might focus on the words: "Let *Eihwaz* serve as a reminder that two people can disagree and still treat each other with respect." If you have had a particularly trying or exhilarating day, before going to bed you might draw another Rune for a report on how well you handled yourself. This practice is an effortless way for you to familiarize yourself with the Runes. At the same time, it teaches you to watch for patterns that come up during certain periods in your life.

Some people prefer a more formal approach to Rune casting—lighting a candle, meditating or saying a prayer before addressing the Oracle. Know, however, that you can always consult the Runes without any special preparation, for it is your desire for clarity that brings the energy of the Runes into play. And keep in mind that you *are* in the realm of play—sacred play—so be open to surprises.

Appropriate Issues

Without resorting to a "yes/no" question, focus on the issue that is troubling you and draw a Rune from your bag. Notice that we speak here of *issues* rather than *questions*. A question would be: "Should I end this relationship?" Translated into an issue, the question becomes a statement: "The issue is my relationship." This seemingly small distinction is actually quite significant. For when the Oracle comments on your issue, rather than telling you what to do, it leaves you free to determine for yourself what constitutes right action in the situation.

As a rule, a single sentence or phrase from the Interpretation will supply you with a useful thought, a fresh idea, or even the necessary coordinates for making a course adjustment in your life. If, however, after reading the Interpretation you still feel unclear, you can always draw a second Rune for clarification.

When no specific issue comes to mind, yet you are drawn to consult the Runes, ask: *What do I need to know for my life now?*

How Often to Use the Runes

How frequently you consult the Runes Oracle is a personal matter. Yet this much is true of most people's experience: there will be times in your life when you use the Runes daily, and other times when you feel no need for them at all. When you find yourself under pressure, know that the Oracle is always there to support you.

DRAWING A SINGLE RUNE

A particularly good time to consult the Runes is when you are facing a challenging situation and could use the advice of a trustworthy friend. With your issue clearly in mind:

1. Reach into the bag and draw out a stone.

2. Look up the Rune's picture and page number on the inside cover of this book.

3. Read the Interpretation, paying close attention to those words or phrases that speak directly to your issue.

Spending a few quiet moments to pick a Rune and read its Interpretation can provide you with a fresh perspective. In practical terms, what you are doing is inviting your mind to function at an intuitive level—the level at which you access your own deep wisdom.

And remember: sometimes the best decision is to make no decision at all. It is often wise to put your issue on hold until you *know*, without hesitation, the next step to take.

A Reality Check

At any time, in the midst of any situation, drawing a single Rune can be especially helpful when you require a reality check: *How am I doing? What do I need to be aware of? What, if anything, have I left out?* On a long drive or a commute between home and work, drawing a single Rune for guidance—for "a good second opinion"—can serve to reassure you about a course of action you have decided upon.

And one thing more. The Runes seem to possess an uncanny ability to reveal the humor in situations where you may have thought there was none.

To Honor Significant Events

Consult the Oracle to honor significant events in your life and in the lives of those you love. Draw a Rune to celebrate birthdays, graduations, marriages, the birth of a child; to mark anniversaries, the change of seasons, the death of a friend. You may wish to record these special readings in a journal to commemorate the occasion.

To Get Your Bearings

Often, picking a single Rune can serve to mark your path or suggest a new direction for your relationship. On occasion, you may find that the very *name* of the Rune you choose—Intimacy, Passion, Renewal—is so evocative that you won't even turn to the Interpretation.

For example, say the issue is "my need for my partner's appreciation," and you draw ⊠ *Letting Go*. You might understand the Rune to be saying: "How about letting go of your need to be appreciated, and giving yourself credit for the many good things you bring to the relationship."

Sometimes, when you are feeling lost or alone, all it takes to get your bearings is the willingness to pick a Rune and the ability to trust your own judgment.

THREE RUNE SPREAD

Although drawing a single Rune usually provides enough information for you to determine what is right action in a given situation, when a circumstance arises that calls for a more in-depth reading, the *Three Rune Spread* can be most helpful.

With your issue clearly in mind, select three Runes, one at a time, and place them in front of you from left to right. Some people prefer to copy each glyph on a piece of paper, and then replace the stone in their bag before drawing again. That way all 25 Runes are available each time you draw.

Let the first Rune stand for the *Overview of the Situation*, the second for the *Challenge*, and the third for the *Course of Action Called For*. After completing the *Three Rune Spread*, you may also decide to draw a fourth Rune to summarize the essence of the previous three.

Frank, a forty-year-old friend of ours, had arrived at a point in his marriage where he knew it was time to separate or to make some serious changes. He put it simply enough: "The issue is my marriage. What does the Oracle have to say?" The Runes he drew were these:

Overview	Challenge	Action
1	2	3
Letting Go	Respect	Commitment

While reading the Interpretations, he thought about his twelve-year marriage to Eleanor, the many interests they shared, the beautiful home they had worked so hard to renovate. Here is how Frank saw it: "This is about letting go of the ways I've been treating my wife that sabotage our marriage. So what's my biggest challenge? Catching myself when I'm being critical and choosing instead to be kind. And replacing my tendency to lecture with a willingness to listen. Showing Eleanor the respect she deserves so that she can believe that I really *am* committed to our marriage."

Then he drew a fourth stone, a Summary Rune, and got Abundance.

Summary

4

Abundance

The meaning of the Summary Rune puzzled Frank until he had given it some thought. "If I can change how I've been acting, and Eleanor responds in a positive way, there's no telling just how rich, how abundant this relationship could be."

DRAWING A RUNE FOR ANOTHER PERSON

Before you draw a Rune for someone else, ask them to formulate their issue of concern clearly in their mind but not state it aloud. Not knowing their issue eliminates any unconscious bias on your part as you pick a Rune for them and read the Interpretation. Discussing their issue *after* the reading is a good way to confirm the accuracy of the Oracle.

If a distant friend could benefit from a reading, consulting the Runes via telephone or the internet is just as effective as if you were seated across the table from each other in a café.

When you are feeling concerned about the welfare of someone you are unable to contact, focus your mind directly on that person and pick a Rune. More often than not, the Rune you draw will serve to ease your mind. This is a way of communicating without words, of sending a prayer or a blessing—of sending your love instead of your worry.

UPRIGHT AND REVERSED RUNES

Although *The Book of Runes* includes two sets of readings—upright for all 25 stones, and reversed for the 16 that can be read two ways, for example ᛉ and ᛝ—that is not the case here. Regardless of how you pull your Rune from the bag, all the aspects of each Relationship Rune are contained in a single reading.

RUNIC OVERRIDE

For those times when the Rune you draw does not seem to address your issue, it may well be that the Oracle has gone into *Runic Override* and is commenting on something that is actually more relevant to your life at the moment. So whenever you find yourself questioning the rightness of a particular Interpretation, before you pick another Rune, consider the possibility of Runic Override, and be willing to look again.

When, as occasionally happens, you are unable to decide between two equally compelling issues, draw a Rune anyway. The Oracle—that is to say, your own inner knowing—can be counted on to address the issue of most immediate concern.

ORACULAR CROSS TALK

If you are already familiar with Oracles such as the *I Ching*, tarot, *The Medicine Cards*, or another of the Rune books, you might enjoy engaging in *Oracular Cross Talk*—comparing what two different oracular instruments have to say about the same subject. Over the years many people have written to tell us about such experiences. Almost invariably, the two readings complemented each other in subtle, amusing, or surprising ways.

If you were to pick a Relationship Rune and drew Gebo, $\boxtimes$, the Rune of Commitment, you might find it useful to learn that this Rune evolved out of Partnership (*The Book of Runes* and *The Rune Cards*) and Trust (*Healing Runes*). While each version has a different focus and its own message to impart, your reading would be considerably enriched by combining it with the corresponding Interpretations from any of the earlier books.

LENDING YOUR RUNES

When it comes to lending your Runes, do whatever feels right to you. Some people feel comfortable sharing their Runes, others do not. If you are sensitive to energy, you may want to keep one set of Runes for your personal use and have a second bag of stones to share with family and friends.

MAKING YOUR OWN RUNES

Creating sets of Runes for yourself and for others can be a gratifying meditation. Pebbles smoothed by a favourite stream or beach glass tumbled by the sea make beautiful Runes. Some people cut Runes from the branches of fruit trees and then burn or carve the glyphs into the wood. Over the years, we have used

Runes made from quartz crystal, amethyst, jade, deer antlers and petrified walrus teeth, with the Runic symbols painted, engraved or scrimshawed on the surface. One potter we know kept a daub of clay from each stone and then formed the Blank Rune from the daubs. You can even fashion an instant set of Runes by cutting 25 rectangles from a piece of cardboard, then marking the glyphs onto them with a felt-tip pen. So when it comes to making a set of Runes, let your passion and your imagination be your guides and have a good time while you are at it.

KEEPING A RUNE JOURNAL

As you begin your exploration of the Relationship Runes, you may find it useful to record the Runes you draw in a journal. Note the time and date, the conditions in your life at the moment and, in a few words, write down whatever message you got from the Rune you picked. Recording your readings is a good way both to acquaint yourself with the Oracle and to evaluate its usefulness as a tool for self-counselling.

At times you may find the same Rune showing up in your readings again and again. It's as if the Oracle were saying, *This is where you need to do your work right now, so pay attention!* Keeping a Rune journal enables you to identify recurring patterns, and the issues to which they relate, as you progress on the journey of relationship.

Council Runes Journal

If you decide to record the Runes you draw during Council (see Chapter 7, Runes Council), you will, in effect, be creating a record of the issues that come up between you and your partner over time. Eventually you will come to see the evolving portrait of your relationship with its difficulties and joys, its growth and transformation.

Dream Journal

Without focusing on an issue, pick a Rune before going to bed, and mark the glyph in your journal. When you wake up, record any remembered dreams, and then consider how the Rune you picked the night before speaks to the content of those dreams.

ONE PERSON'S PRACTICE

When our friend Alex, a musician and computer wizard, bought the first edition of *The Book of Runes* in 1982, he decided to work with only the Interpretations for a year before reading the rest of the text. He began his day by drawing a Rune and asking: "What key is this day written in?" Then, before bed, he would ask, "How was my playing today?" meaning, how well did he meet the challenges of the day.

He kept his bag of Runes and set of Interpretations (photocopied, laminated and strung on a chain) on the seat of his car and often picked Runes while he drove, discussing new ideas with the Oracle, inquiring after distant friends, and sometimes even asking for clues to the sixth race at Santa Anita. Eventually he knew the Interpretations so well that when he drew a Rune he had no need to read the text. When last we heard from him, he was "using my mind as a random number generator, just spinning the Runes till one comes up."

Whether you are coming to the Relationship Runes as a novice or as a long-time friend of the Oracle, it is our hope that this latest evolution of the Runes will prove to be a reliable and trustworthy compass for the heart. Whenever you find yourself at a crossroads in your life, or when your intention is to act for the highest good of all concerned, know that the Runes Oracle is available to serve you.

The essence of our being is love.

Health is inner peace. Healing is letting go of fear.

Giving and receiving are the same.

We can let go of the past and of the future.

Now is the only time there is and each instant is for giving.

We can learn to love ourselves and others by forgiving rather than judging.

We can become love finders rather than fault finders.

We can choose and direct ourselves to be peaceful inside regardless of what is happening outside.

We are students and teachers to each other.

We can focus on the whole of life rather than the fragments.

We can always perceive ourselves and others as either extending love or giving a call for help.

Since love is eternal, death need not be viewed as fearful.

Center For Attitudinal Healing
Sausalito, California

——— 5 ———
SOME USEFUL
TECHNIQUES

*It isn't always what you say, but the way you say it. One
marriage counsellor sometimes asks couples who have
difficulty communicating, to forget words and take 20 minutes
and simply look into each other's eyes and be silent together.
They may see what they have missed: Longing hearts,
unfulfilled dreams, unmet needs, or a yearning to love and be
loved. They learn that deep communication is more than words.*
—Stephen Levine, *A Year to Live*

*A wonderful marriage doesn't make life easy or painless. It
just makes the work sweeter and the pain more meaningful.*
—David Schnarch, *Passionate Marriage*

Evolving as they have out of a spiritual tradition more than
2,000 years old, the Relationship Runes can act to awaken,
support and strengthen the sacred nature of relationship itself.
The Runes make possible a kind of sacred play in which the victory

belongs to all who open their hearts to the mystery of meaningful relationships. Whatever your issue may be, the exercises and layouts that follow call you to have life more abundantly.

RUNE AFFIRMATIONS

It has taken more than two decades to develop the three sets of Interpretations that are the sum and substance of *The Book of Runes*, *RuneCards*, *Healing Runes*, and *Relationship Runes*. When you read the categories as they appear on the inside front cover of this book, you will see that, in most cases, there is a clear progression from one Interpretation to the next. Recently, while working with the Interpretations, we discovered we could pick a Rune for an issue, and then create a one-sentence affirmation from the names of that Rune's three aspects. For example:

Germanic Name	Book of Runes	Healing Runes	Relationship Runes

10 Ⅿ *Algiz*   PROTECTION   BOUNDARIES   MUTUAL TRUST
Affirmation: *We protect our love by honoring each other's boundaries and mutual trust grows between us.*

11 Ⅿ *Fehu*   POSSESSIONS   HONESTY   ABUNDANCE
Affirmation: *With honesty as my most precious possession, I live a life of simple abundance.*

When you are facing a particularly challenging situation, you may find it useful to pick a Rune and craft an affirmation specific to your issue. Or you might enjoy creating a Rune Affirmation for the coming week and writing it in your journal to remind you each day of its message. Tape it to the bathroom mirror, the refrigerator door, the dashboard of your car—any place where it will catch your attention.

You can also take the time to compose a statement that encompasses the essential meaning of all three generations of Rune meanings. Once the affirmations are complete, you will have created a set of 25 flash cards with your personal affirmation on one side and the Rune's three aspects on the other.

16 ⓑ *Berkana*
GROWTH
PRAYER
RIGHT ACTION

*With right action for my compass
and prayer as my companion,
I grow.*

Taken together, these 25 affirmations will provide you with your own set of "direction finders" for those moments when you need a quick course adjustment, a word of encouragement or advice.

UNFINISHED BUSINESS

If you have unfinished business with someone you are unable to contact, or perhaps a friend or loved one who has died, the Runes Oracle can help you to complete whatever remains incomplete between you. Take a moment to visualize the person as you best remember them. Next, make a list of those things you never talked about and now wish you had. Then pick a Rune for each issue. As you read the Interpretations, watch for any words or phrases that sound like something you might expect to hear from the person you are thinking about.

The Runes have an uncanny way of accessing the deep understanding of our hearts and minds. Whatever the case may be, when we hear the voice of truth, we usually recognize it. Letters from people who have worked with the Runes in this way indicate that the results are invariably helpful and comforting.

THE "X" FACTOR

In this exercise, you are asking all 25 Runes to rearrange themselves in an order specific to your issue. If there are two of you, and both of you are willing, the "X" Factor may be undertaken jointly. However, you can always choose to do this layout on your own.

The reading that follows was done by our friend Frank of the Three Rune Spread (see Chapter 4). Six months had passed and, despite his strong desire to resolve the difficulties between them, his marriage with Eleanor was falling apart. "Maybe I just wasn't respectful enough. Or maybe I didn't change my behaviour fast enough. Now Eleanor wants one of us to move out, and I really need some good advice." Frank decided to give the "X" Factor a try, the obvious issue being his marriage.

To begin, he placed all 25 stones face down and, using both hands, moved them around until they were well mixed. Then he set them out in five rows with the glyphs still hidden.

One by one, Frank turned the stones glyph-side up. Here is the way the Oracle presented itself.

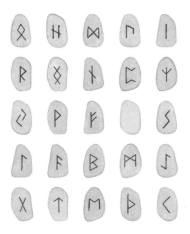

Next he isolated the nine Runes that formed the "X" in his layout.

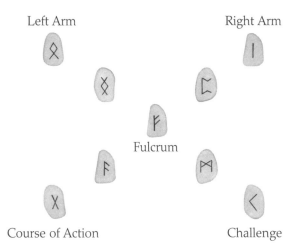

Left Arm

Right Arm

Fulcrum

Course of Action

Challenge

As he studied the formation more closely, Frank realized that he was actually looking at the Rune *Gebo*, which originally meant"a gift."Then it dawned on him that like three generations under one roof, ⊠, the Rune of *Partnership, Trust,* and *Commitment* formed the framework on which to build a loving relationship.

And there, in the centre of it all—at the fulcrum of loving relationship itself—was his old friend ᛖ, *Abundance*, signalling for his attention once again. And not just once, but twice, since it had positioned itself as central to both the Challenge and the Course of Action Called for. In that position—as the fulcrum of the "X" Factor—he would be reading its Interpretation twice. Clearly *Abundance*, in some form, was the key to having a loving relationship with Eleanor.

Left Arm: The Challenge

Here is Frank's reading:
"Home & Family ⊠ is where I find my *Renewal* ⊠. And what better form can *Abundance* ᛖ take than practising *Loving Kindness* ᛗ on the road to *Inner Peace* ᚲ."

As Frank read the Interpretations for each of the five Challenge Runes, he began to see more clearly some of the negative patterns of communication that had grown up between him and Eleanor. Recently he had been under tremendous pressure from his boss to complete a long overdue project and was feeling fearful about his job. At the same time, Eleanor was recovering from major surgery. Rather than admitting how stressed and vulnerable they were both feeling, they had taken to attacking each other.

"So, the way to restore abundance to our lives," Frank said, "is to fill our home with feelings of loving kindness, which will lead to inner peace."

Next, Frank turned to the right arm of the *X Factor* to help him understand what could be done to encourage feelings of loving kindness between them.

Right Arm: The Course of Action Called For

"*Reflection* ⏀ is a call to pause and consider what most requires repair and restoration between you. With *Intimacy* ⏀ at a low ebb, in order for *Abundance* ⏀ to once more bless your relationship, you must both work to improve *Communication* ⏀, which will, over time, strengthen the quality of your *Commitment* ⏀ to each other."

As Frank finished reading the Interpretation for ⏀ *Abundance* one last time, he began to see why this particular Rune kept reoccurring in his readings about his marriage. Since receiving the Rune of Abundance is always a reminder to count your blessings, it became obvious that he and Eleanor were *both* guilty of focusing on what was *wrong* with their relationship rather than being grateful for and acknowledging what was right. Eleanor and Frank had both become so caught up in their own issues that they had lost sight of what a loving relationship was all about.

If he and Eleanor truly wanted to renew their marriage, it was time to take the words of the Oracle to heart and begin acting on them: *Wishing nothing to be different than it is at this present moment is to invite abundance into your life. The ability to take joy in each other when life is difficult is a true sign of abundance.*

HEART BREATHING

Heart Breathing is a gift from Emerald Starr, a dear friend who sent us this exercise from Ubud, Bali. He wrote:

"All of us go through slumps from time to time. It's just part of the natural rhythm of life. So when my energy is in a downward spiral and things are looking bleak, I take a moment and *focus all my awareness in my heart*. I feel the muscle expand as I breathe in… I feel it contract as I breathe out… and the next thing I know, *I am breathing with my heart*.

"A meditation that has helped me enormously is heart breathing while holding an image in my mind of someone I love, or something I feel deep gratitude for. Doing this meditation somehow brings things back into perspective so I can identify the unmet emotional needs that usually come disguised as self-righteous anger, resentment, or despair. This simple practice almost always lifts me out of my misery within minutes.

"What's more, heart breathing also has the surprising effect of clearing the energy of people around me. If anyone nearby is creating a disruption, when I start breathing with my heart, I've noticed that they either stop being disruptive or just go away."

Heart Breathing Rune Meditation

Seat yourself comfortably, close your eyes, and begin breathing with your heart. When you are ready, focus on some aspect of your life that calls for *forgiveness, releasing or embracing*.

Now draw a Rune from your bag. Say you get ⟨⟩, the Rune of Perseverance. As you read the Interpretation, continue breathing with your heart, letting go of all judgment, all resistance to change. Breathe in the energy of perseverance until you feel it in your heart, carrying with it the certain knowledge that this Rune represents your ability and willingness to see things through to completion. As you breathe out, release all resistance to doing what needs to be done. Forgive yourself for the time it is taking to complete your task, and know that you *always* possess the freedom both to persevere and to begin again.

In the stillness of meditation, continue heart breathing until you are ready to open your eyes and fully embrace this present moment—refreshed, filled with gratitude and open to new possibilities.

Ancient as they are, the Runes remain a flexible and open-ended system. In time, you are bound to discover new and creative ways to use and benefit from them. So enjoy your Runes, play with them, let them teach you to listen to the wise voice within. We at the RuneWorks always appreciate hearing from you about your experiences with the Oracle, and about any new spreads or techniques that occur to you.

No one can persuade another to change.
Each of us guards a gate of change that can
only be opened from the inside. We cannot open
the gate of another, either by argument or by
emotional appeal.

—Marilyn Ferguson

— 6 —
CALLING "TIME OUT!"

Choose curiosity over opinion,
Choose understanding over self-defence,
Choose building relationship over scoring points,
Choose mutual trust over doubt,
Choose being truthful over being right.

—Robert Ott

Gratitude is not only the greatest of virtues,
it is the parent of all others.

—Cicero

Time Out Therapy, as our friend Emma calls it, is useful in any situation where feelings are running high. Over the years, she has learned to employ "the pause that refreshes" in work situations as well as in her primary relationship. "Rarely do I leap to judgment anymore," Emma told us. "When I realize that I don't know how to deal with a particular situation, I usually remember to back off, which almost always allows space for unexpected solutions to present themselves. My challenge is to avoid becoming paralysed by all the fears, hopes and expectations that overwhelm me when I get caught up in the future or stuck in the past. I'm really learning the value of just staying present, and of taking the time to pause in the present moment."

All major contact sports include some provision for calling "Time Out." What is vital in the arena of relationship is the willingness and ability to stop and take a break *before* tempers flare and strong words lead to emotional or even physical violence. As a strategy, we have found that there is nothing to equal the simple act of taking a time out.

Practice Sessions

Begin by choosing a special word or a phrase like "Cut!" or "Time Out!" or adopting a hand signal such as the "T" used by coaches and athletes. The next step is to practise calling for a time out when things are going well between you. That way the technique will be familiar when hurt feelings or misunderstandings trigger an outburst of anger. We suggest that you make it your intention to become proficient in this kind of "cease-fire drill."

Early Warning Signals

Pay attention to warning signs like rising voices, harsh tones, a racing heart or a churning stomach. Sentences that begin with "You make me feel," as well as the intrusion of "always" and "never" usually indicate that your conversation is about to be derailed by judgment, criticism or blame. At times like these, the "T" signal is particularly useful since it is immediate, visual and requires no words.

Going to a Neutral Corner

A Time Out usually calls for you to separate for an agreed upon length of time. However, if either of you is still too angry or too raw to resume your discussion when you come back together, you can always extend the Time Out.

No Self-Medicating

By self-medicating, we mean anything that might artificially shift or alter your mood, including alcohol, drugs or over-indulging in food. Self-medication is a way of avoiding facing difficult realizations, or numbing ourselves against the pain of our feelings.

Triangulation

Although we often turn to our friends for support when we are feeling upset or angry, it is important to resist the urge to involve any third party during a Time Out. Time Out means time by yourself, cooling down time. And while you are alone, do your best to avoid building a case against your partner. One useful technique is to focus on your breathing in order to stay present. Here are the words of Buddhist teacher Thich Nhat Hanh, words that we find helpful:

> *Breathing in, I calm body and mind.*
> *Breathing out, I smile.*
> *Dwelling in the present moment.*
> *This is the only moment.*

Repeat these words to yourself a number of times and you'll see what a difference they make.

The Sweat Factor

Walk, swim, go for a run or a bike ride. Weed the garden, scrub some floors or clean the attic. Do whatever it takes to work up a sweat and get your endorphins flowing. Physical activity keeps you in your body and out of your head, while helping you to discharge some of the tension which is built up during an unpleasant exchange.

Writing it Down

Unspoken agreements are the cause of much mischief and misunderstanding in meaningful relationships. When both of you are committed to working out your differences, writing down the rules for your Time Outs is always a good idea (see page 66).

Consulting the Oracle

During your time alone, each of you might draw a Rune to help you get your bearings. Focus on an issue, or on the good of the Relationship itself, and ask: "What is right action in this situation?" Then draw a Rune from your bag. If what you read in the Interpretation helps you to shift your perspective by even a few degrees, it can make a real difference in your attitude and in your behaviour.

Resuming Your Discussion

If either of you still needs more space, be willing to agree to another Time Out. When you finally resume your discussion, hopefully you will find yourselves in a much better place. Your intention is to acquire new communication skills that will serve you, your partner and the Relationship. So be kind to one another, remembering that "mistakes" often contain valuable information about how to do things differently next time.

Closure

Each time you confront and successfully deal with a serious issue in this way, the bond between you will be renewed and strengthened.

Summary

• Whoever feels their anger rising gives the "T" signal to communicate their need for a time out.
• Separate for one hour and do something physically active.
• No drugs or alcohol during the break.
• No phone calls or e-mailing. However, if either of you really needs a good second opinion, feel free to pick a Rune.
• When you check in, unless you are both ready to reconnect, agree on another Time Out.
• Finally, share with each other something useful you have learned from the process.

Every relationship we are in is a reflection of

the relationship we have with ourselves.

If I like myself, if I trust myself,

then the liking and the trusting

will be echoed in my relationship with you.

—Akshara Noor

RUNES COUNCIL

*God gave us two ears and only one mouth, that we
should listen twice as much as we speak.*

—Ancient Proverb

*Have you ever noticed what happens when you really
listen to another person, listen without reacting or even
the intention to respond, listen without being influenced by
long-held images and memories or firmly held positions,
listen instead with a beginner's mind and the ears of a
child hearing a bedtime story?*

—Jack Zimmerman and Virginia Coyle
The Way of Council

W hen did you last feel listened to in such a way that you
knew the person listening really got where you were
coming from, truly understood your motives, your concerns and
fears? And when did you last listen to someone in such a way
that they knew, without a doubt, that they had been heard and

acknowledged? It is easy to overlook the fact that *the most effective way to improve any relationship is to change the way we listen and speak to one another*.

Deep listening is a spiritual act. So is speaking the truth. However, changing life-long communication habits requires patience, discipline, and a lot of practice. Interactions that are honest and compassionate must be committed to and employed consistently. When we do so, new neural pathways are created in the brain—as well as new pathways for the heart. As we learn to express our concerns in direct, kind, and non-accusatory ways, we are also learning to nurture and heal our relationships. One well-respected method that supports this kind of healing by creating a safe space in which to explore our differences is a practice known as Council.

COUNCIL METHOD

The origins of Council can be traced to the customs of Native American tribal peoples, in particular the League of the Iroquois, the People of the Plains and the Southwestern Pueblos. Council was used in ceremony, to reach consensus and to settle disputes. A contemporary form of Council is found in a therapeutic technique known as "Co-counselling," where two people take turns listening intently to each other's issues of concern without responding or commenting.

Council Method, as it is presented here, was first developed and taught by Jack Zimmerman and Virginia Coyle at the Ojai Foundation in California, where it is practised regularly by the Board of Directors, the staff, and by groups of people working together on the land or attending conferences. The method is described in Zimmerman and Coyle's pioneering work, *The Way of Council.*

Although Council Method is traditionally undertaken by groups of people, since the focus of this book is meaningful relationships, we can offer the following guidelines for any two people who wish to nourish, restore or deepen their relationship.

RUNES COUNCIL

Preparation

Although a Runes Council can be held at any time, evening is usually best. Turn off the phone, send the kids to bed, remove the pets from the room—whatever it takes to create a quiet and soothing atmosphere for you both. Council is always a special occasion, so do your best to make it feel that way.

You will need four things: a candle and "talking piece," your bag of Runes and your book. The talking piece can be anything that holds personal meaning for you—your grandfather's pocket watch, a gift made by a child, a lovely seashell.

Dim the lights and seat yourselves on comfortable chairs or cushions on the floor. Include in your circle a third chair or cushion on which to place your bag of Runes and book. By performing this act, you are creating a space for "the Third," the voice of the Relationship itself. Recognizing and honoring the presence of the Third renders the Council circle sacred.

Opening the Runes Council

Place the unlit candle and the talking piece in the centre of the circle. Now close your eyes and sit for a few moments in silence. Relax and breathe deeply as you separate yourself from the activities and concerns of the day. When you are ready, open your eyes and acknowledge each other's presence.

Next, one of you lights the candle and offers a prayer in silence or out loud. The burning candle represents both the innocence of the human heart and the transformative power of Council.

Start with a "Check-In"

Decide between you who will speak first, then pick up the talking piece and begin. It often helps to start with a check-in. Perhaps you have a story to share, or you might simply want to say that you're feeling good or exhausted or that you had a difficult day at work. When either of you brings up a thorny issue ("I'm feeling uncomfortable about the argument we had over dinner...") it is best to employ "I" statements in order to avoid falling into criticism or blame. When you have both finished checking in, return the talking piece to the centre of the circle. Now you are ready to begin.

On the next page you will find a set of guidelines for your Runes Council:

RUNES COUNCIL GUIDELINES

1. When either of you calls for a Council, that call becomes a priority in your life.

2. Remember that you always come together as equals when you sit in the circle of Council.

3. Listen attentively, from a place of stillness, to what your partner is saying. Let go of any need to think about what you will say next.

4. Speak from and listen with your heart.

5. Be brief. Do your best to bring up one issue at a time in order to avoid overwhelming your partner.

6. Never interrupt. When the talking piece is passed to you, or returned to the centre, then it is your time to speak.

7. What is shared in Council is not discussed outside the circle.

8. If you and your partner decide to make Council an ongoing part of your relationship, agree to sit together regularly.

THE FOUR RUNES COUNCIL

We have found drawing four Runes to be an effective way to use the Oracle in the service of Council. The first three Runes stand for the following: (1) *Issue of Concern*, (2) *The Call*, and (3) *Appropriate Action Called For*. The fourth Rune represents the *Voice of the Relationship Itself*.

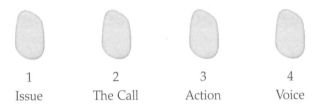

| 1 | 2 | 3 | 4 |
| Issue | The Call | Action | Voice |

The First Council Rune

First, agree on your *Issue of Concern*, then state it aloud. For example:"The issue is our lack of time alone together."Now pick a Rune to comment on that issue.

If, however, no particular issue comes to mind, simply ask, *What do we need to consider, right now, for the well-being of our relationship?* Allow the Rune you draw to identify the *Issue of Concern* for this Council.

As you read the Rune Interpretation aloud, notice which words and phrases apply to your situation, letting them serve as jumping-off points for your own thoughts and feelings.

Say you draw Rune 5, ᚢ, *Uruz*, the Rune of Support. Ask yourself whether you feel listened to, cared for, criticized or ignored in your relationship. Whatever the case may be, *Uruz* counsels you to ask directly for what you need and to encourage your partner to do the same. Take no offence, keep your heart open, and support one another in this process.

Whoever is ready to speak first picks up the talking piece and begins, remembering to be brief in order to avoid overwhelming the other with too much information at one time. When you have finished speaking, place the talking piece between you so that your Council partner may respond. Continue taking turns—remembering never to interrupt, no matter how great the urge—giving your full attention as you listen, and allowing each other the space to absorb what is being said. When both of you feel complete, return the first Rune to the bag.

While Council is simple in concept, it can be somewhat challenging in practice. Inevitably there will be times when one of you falls back into old patterns of negative communication. You may even experience surges of intense emotion that surface without warning. The call then is for honesty, integrity, and for bearing in mind that no negative pattern can be perpetuated unless *both* of you support it.

The Second Council Rune

When you feel you have reached a deeper understanding of your issue, and you are ready to move to the next level, let the person who did not draw the first Rune draw a second and read the Interpretation aloud. This second Rune represents the *The Call*, an invitation to open the lines of communication between you and explore your differences.

Say you draw Rune 18, $\mathbb{N}$, *Laguz*, the Rune of Change. *Laguz* speaks to our willingness to accept change gracefully—our ability to be flexible, to modify habitual behaviours, and to grow.

As you take turns sharing your intentions, thoughts and feelings, the steps you need to take to support one another—and the Relationship—will become clearer to you. When you are ready to move on, place the talking piece in the centre of the circle and return the Rune to its bag.

The Third Council Rune

The third Rune stands for the *Appropriate Action* called for in this situation. Say you choose Rune 9, $\lceil \rceil$, *Eihwaz*, the Rune of Respect. In the Interpretation you will read: "Respect in action is demonstrated by the care we take in appreciating what is important to those we love." Respect of this kind is shown quite simply by your willingness to continue discussing an issue until you can both agree on what constitutes right action. And since respect is always a two-way street, it is good to remember: "Where there is mutual respect—regardless of differing desires, opinions, values, or beliefs—love will prevail." More than anything else, this Rune is saying, respect is the firmest footing for love.

The talking piece continues to pass between you until neither of you have anything more to add. Then return the third Rune to the bag.

The Fourth Council Rune

By drawing the fourth or *Summary Rune*, you are inviting the Relationship to communicate to you *its* needs, *its* dreams. At this point, one of you moves to the third cushion and takes a Rune from the bag. While reading the Interpretation, a subtle shift in awareness may occur, a shift that takes you out of the power struggle of "your way" versus "my way," and opens you instead to a "third way"—one that allows both of you to consider what is best for your Relationship itself.

Say you draw Rune 12, ⫠, *Wunjo*, the Rune of Celebration. A blend of joy, serenity and delight, *Wunjo* encourages you to make celebration a part of your daily practice. So take this Rune as a reminder to celebrate what is nourishing and pleasing in your life. And remember to ask yourself any time you are facing a difficult situation: *Is what I want and how I am behaving good for the relationship?*

Closing the Council

When both of you have said what you needed to say and feel that you have been heard, place the talking piece between you and return the last Rune to the bag. Next, take a moment to consider how the essence of the four Runes chosen during this council can be combined in a single statement about your issue.

1	2	3	4
Uruz,	*Laguz*	*Eihwaz*	*Wunjo*
Support	Change	Respect	Celebration

It might be said this way: *As we learn to support each other's right to change and grow, a deepening respect between us will indeed be cause for celebration.*

Finally, repeat out loud the affirmation found at the end of the Rune of Respect: *The Divine in me recognizes and bows to the Divine in you.* Now bow to each other and blow out the candle.

This concludes the Runes Council.

Over the Horizon Council

Once this practice becomes a regular part of your life, it is worth remembering that you can do Council even when you are far apart. A couple we know has become proficient at what they call "Over-the-Horizon Council." These Councils take place either by phone or e-mail, usually on a Sunday night, on the boundary between the old week and the new.

Each of them lights a candle, and after agreeing on their issue and deciding who will speak first, they begin. When one of them finishes speaking, they simply say, "Now you," and the virtual talking piece passes between them. No one interrupts, the dialogue is lean, the usual rules of Council apply.

Integrating Council Method into the fabric of your life will, over time, provide you with satisfying new ways of listening and communicating. In fact, even when no particular issue is calling for your attention, the simple act of sitting in Council, drawing a Rune, and then discussing what comes up for you, can bring you to a more peaceful, loving place.

> *From the highest possible place*
> *and for the greatest possible good,*
> *we dedicate the merit of this practice.*

Promised

I have prayed for what I needed

Giving thanks for what I had

My soul and heart are seeded

Thoughts of harvest make me glad

We are born of wind and water

We are promised to the sky

I have loved you since I found you

I will love you till I die

—R.B.

— 8 —
THE JOURNEY OF RELATIONSHIP

We are not held back by the love we didn't receive in the past, but by the love we're not extending in the present.
—Marianne Williamson, *A Return to Love*

What is the particular gift this day has given me? Who have I loved, and have I dared to love them as well as I could? Have I contributed to the well-being of another, have I enhanced their sense of dignity or expanded the possibilities of their lives? Have I flown as close to the fire at the heart of the mysteries of love and knowledge as I dare? And of everything I have received, have I given anything back?
—Richard Thieme, *Islands in the Clickstream*

The Interpretations that make up the final part of this book are all you really need to begin your journey with the Relationship Runes. When you consult the Oracle, a single question, a simple prayer, will always suffice: *Show me what I need to know for my life now?*

Wherever you find yourself at this present moment—whether deeply in love, alone after ending a relationship, a single parent caring for a child—it is important to recognize that the fabric of our lives is woven from caring relationships of many kinds. So if you draw a Rune, read the words "partner" or "marriage" in the Interpretation, and find yourself thinking, "I'm not in a committed relationship so this Rune doesn't apply to me," take a moment to consider all the people with whom you *do* enjoy meaningful relationships. Then ask yourself: "How does this Interpretation apply to my issue?"

When you turn to the Runes for counsel, it is good to remember that rather than depending on the Oracle to solve your problems for you, *you are asking to be pointed in the direction where you will discover answers for yourself.* While there are no simple explanations concerning the nature of the Runes and how they function, one thing is certain: *The energy that engages them is your own and, ultimately, the wisdom as well.*

So it is that wherever meaningful relationships once existed, presently flourish, or are just coming into being, *Relationship Runes: A Compass for the Heart* looks to be of service.

Love one another,

but make not a bond of love:

let it rather be a moving sea

between the shores of your souls.

Fill each other's cup

but drink not from one cup.

Give one another of your bread,

but eat not from the same loaf.

Sing and dance together and be joyous,

but let each one of you be alone

even as the strings of a lute are alone

but they quiver with the same music.

—Khalil Gibran, *The Prophet*

─── 9 ───
INTERPRETATIONS

1   LOVING KINDNESS

Mannaz

*A correct relationship to your self is primary, for
from it flow all possible right relationships with
others and with the Divine.*

                    —*The Book of Runes*, The Self

*Use this day to simplify your life. Bring harmony
where you find dissonance and balance where
there is none.*

                    —*Healing Runes*, Innocence

In the ancient runic tradition, *Mannaz* stood for a man and a
woman and, by extension, all humankind. In the context of
meaningful relationships, this Rune represents the open-
hearted, generous treatment of ourselves and others.

Since forgiveness and acceptance form the foundation of
loving kindness, receiving *Mannaz* is a reminder to make
forgiveness a guiding principle for your life. For without the
ability and willingness to forgive, how can we ever truly love

86

ourselves or fully love another? When you can look openly and honestly at your relationships, both past and present, and forgive without exception, that is loving kindness in action.

We all carry within us critical and unkind voices that are the cause of much pain, resentment and guilt. Let us begin, this Rune is saying, by forgiving one another for being human and for making so many mistakes. When seen from another perspective, a mistake is actually valuable information that allows us to do things differently next time. And so we learn.

Accepting the things you cannot change includes pardoning yourself for the hurt you may have caused others, and then taking the necessary steps to make amends. Ask for forgiveness face to face, in writing or through prayer. Do whatever it takes. The ability to have compassion for ourselves, as well as for others, allows us to let go of the past and to move on with an easy mind and a peaceful spirit. For it is only by relinquishing the past that we are able to experience a true present.

Like many of life's essentials, loving kindness begins at home. So instead of being intent on changing, or becoming a better person, know that *showing loving kindness for yourself is about befriending who you already are*. If you pay close attention, you will come to realize that the very behaviour you criticize and judge in others is often a mirror of your own actions. As you learn to be more gentle and honest with yourself, acts of loving kindness will become the natural expression of who you are.

In truth, there need be nothing selfish about self-love. It is simply what is required of us with the commandment to "Love thy neighbour as thyself." For as we learn to love ourselves, we also grow in our ability to give and receive love. Whenever you extend your love outward to another, without conditions or expectations, you are practising loving kindness.

If you take the Rune of Loving Kindness and cut it down the middle, what you have is the Rune of Celebration with its mirror image. So enjoy yourself, *Mannaz* is saying. Love and accept yourself just as you are, and you will begin to notice changes in all your relationships.

If someone you love is going through a difficult period, sometimes the most valuable help you can give is simply to listen, do your best to understand, and offer support and encouragement. Let them know that you believe wholeheartedly in their ability to work things out for themselves. This, too, is loving kindness in action.

We all know what a kind act feels like and that its nature is benevolent. An act of kindness frees up energy and promotes healing by allowing the river of life force to flow around any obstacle. Through the practice of loving kindness we come to understand that, in truth, we are all the same heart beating.

> *I encourage, I accept, I forgive—*
> *In all that I do, I practise loving kindness.*

2   # COMMITMENT

Gebo

> *True partnership is achieved only by separate and*
> *whole beings who retain their separateness even*
> *as they unite. Remember to let the winds of heaven*
> *dance between you.*
>
> —*The Book of Runes*, Partnership

> *Trust is the foundation upon which we build our lives*
> *and do God's work in the world.*
>
> —*Healing Runes*, Trust

In the ancient runic tradition, *Gebo* signified a gift—a gift given by the Norse gods to humankind, or gifts bestowed by chieftains upon their loyal followers. In the context of meaningful relationships, this translates as the gifts we give to one another, gifts of love, respect and trust upon which to build a life together.

With this Rune we are in the province of the faithful heart. When you say to your partner, "I am committed to you," it is a declaration that the two of you are now "we." It is a pledge that you are prepared to give this relationship everything you've got—your love, your attention, your respect, your willingness to do whatever it takes to work things out in times of difficulty.

Although the inability to commit is a common problem, so is committing too soon. Sometimes passion and its attendant fantasies lure us into making a commitment to someone we hardly know. And while it is possible to get lucky, don't count on it. Give yourselves time to get to know each other in some depth before you commit.

What makes for a lasting relationship in these times of turbulent change? Since the quality of our agreements determines the strength of any enduring relationship, begin by making clear agreements. Sit together, with expert help if need be, and establish your priorities. Then write down your intentions and goals, making certain that important conditions, boundaries and obligations are acceptable to you both.

When two people are committed to building a relationship, their first agreement must be to never intentionally hurt one another. And yet we are all human, we all make mistakes. So if you are feeling a strong emotional reaction to something your partner has said or done, rather than withdrawing, going on the attack, or defending yourself, take the time to consider your own role in what has happened. Ask yourself: Why am I so angry? Why am I feeling so hurt? What is this situation telling me about myself? *Take the intensity of your own reaction as compelling evidence that something unresolved within you is calling for your attention and needs to be lifted into the light of understanding.*

All too often, it is our *unspoken* agreements—expectations we take for granted, assumptions we fail to discuss—that cause resentments to build. So if the needle is edging into the red, begin by letting go of your need to be right. Then speak from your heart and listen with your heart. Explore together how the two of you got off track. What you learn will help you to do things differently from now on.

If, however, the present challenge brings up painful memories of past failures, take heart and say to yourself: *That was then, and this is now, and I am not that person anymore.*

For some of us, receiving *Gebo* is a call to evaluate the quality of our present commitment. Do you feel cherished? Do you cherish your partner? Do both of you continue to honor your vows or are they dying of neglect? Although it sometimes takes courage to share with your partner the truth of what you are feeling, the ability and willingness to do so is to honor the Relationship.

And while this Rune both encourages and supports commitment, it also carries a warning against collapsing yourselves into one another. So be mindful to give your partner the freedom to explore who they are in the world—without jealousy, without the need for them to change or do things differently. Once again, remember to let the winds of heaven dance between you.

Commitment to one another is the essential first step in establishing a lasting relationship. It is the foundation for marriage. And yet what you are actually committing to is *the sacred nature of relationship itself.* So be grateful for the support and opportunities for growth that union with your beloved brings. When you hold fast to your partner in loyalty and respect, the heart of relationship is full, nourishment is everywhere, and even the ordinary brings a blessing.

> *In faith and love*
> *I renew my commitment to you*
> *this day.*

3   COMMUNICATION

Ansuz

You may be concerned over what appears to be
failed communication, lack of clarity, or awareness.
Remember that what is happening is timely to your
process. If the well is clogged, this is the moment
for cleaning out the old.

—*The Book of Runes*, Signals

For those who seek to heal situations from the past—
for what was done or left undone—this Rune counsels
you to open your heart and act.

—*Healing Runes*, Guilt

In the ancient runic tradition, *Ansuz* stood for the mouth of a river and for the mouth as a source of utterances. In the context of meaningful relationships, this Rune supports our ability to connect with, listen to and understand one another.

A loving relationship is created over time by the sharing of experiences, by honoring the differences between you, and by your willingness to support each other's dreams. For all this to occur, listening with and speaking from the heart is essential. Listening from the heart—that is to say sympathetic, active listening—is a life preserver in the white water of meaningful relationships. Therefore take *Ansuz* as a reminder to listen with courtesy, sensitivity and, equally important, without interrupting.

Since relationships are fertile ground for misunderstandings and conflict, it is only natural for two people who love each other to have serious disagreements from time to time. Keep in mind that difficult truths are easier to take in small doses. Make a commitment with your partner—or anyone with whom you have a caring relationship—to stay present, to be brief, and to show respect by hearing each other out.

Sometimes when you receive the Rune of Communication, you are simply being reminded to check in with one another. When was the last time you really talked? Is there some sensitive issue you are avoiding? Whatever the case may be, many people find it useful to set aside a special time to discuss what is happening in their lives—the successes and the joys, the losses and the sorrows. Intimacy thrives when we share with each other what we are experiencing and feeling.

If you find yourself under pressure, pay close attention to your tone of voice, for tone is often more telling than words. Is your voice free of impatience and irritation? Free of judgments and expectations? When your tone is critical, or if you continue to bring up the past during discussions of the present, it will be difficult for the other person to avoid feeling defensive or to really hear what you are saying.

Invariably there will be times when communication breaks

down, leaving one or both of you frustrated, angry or in pain. When either of you is upset by the words or actions of the other, rather than withdrawing or going on the attack, make a conscious effort to express clearly what you are feeling. If, however, the emotions between you are already too strong to allow for rational discussion, it may be helpful to *simply agree to disagree,* call time out, and come together again when you have both calmed down.

And then there is the gift of humor. When laughter and humor are an integral part of your relationship, they can serve as medicine for healing what ails you. So remember to laugh at yourself and to look for the humor in tense situations. Being able to laugh at the same things—at least some of the time—is vital to the health of any meaningful relationship.

Whatever your issue may be, know that, in time, this too shall pass. And while situations change, the goal remains the same: to listen always with your heart, to speak always from your heart. How wonderful to be listened to in this manner. How nourishing to be spoken to in this way.

> *When I speak, I speak from my heart.*
> *When you speak, I listen with my heart.*

4 HOME & FAMILY

Othila

*Consider not only what will benefit you, but also
what will benefit others.*

—*The Book of Runes*, Separation

*Receiving this Rune calls us to spend a moment in
prayer for the relief of pain, the practice of kindness,
and the restoration of peace in our troubled world.*

—*Healing Runes*, Grief

In the ancient runic tradition, *Othila* stood for one's native land, home and inheritance. In the context of meaningful relationships, this Rune represents the home we make in order to nourish intimacy and create a family.

L ike a great and ancient tree, *Othila* shelters generations beneath its spreading branches. In its shade, we embrace our traditions and honor our roots. A Rune of continuity and survival, ideally it embodies a safe haven where life is predictable and no harm can come to us. Home is where we take our rest, and even when we are on our own, we can always make a home for ourselves.

Receiving this Rune, take a few moments to honor your family of origin, your ancestors, their values, and traditions. What do we mean by family values? Simple virtues such as loyalty, dependability, honesty, doing your share, concern for the safety and well-being of the children, a passion for the Divine. What a blessing it is when you can go to an elder for comfort and council. And what a pleasure it is to make your own experience available to the young, who so often show us ways and truths we might otherwise miss entirely.

And yet to discover the broader meaning of family, what Hawaiians call *ohana*, we must look beyond blood, beyond marriage, and gratefully acknowledge the people to whom we are drawn by mutual interest, the ones who comfort us when we are sick, those with whom we choose to share what we hold dear.

If you and your partner are considering whether or not to marry and have children, it is essential that you discuss your feelings openly and honestly with one another, since a "Yes" will change your lives forever. In your evolution from a loving couple to a family with children, intimacy and privacy will often be replaced by nurturing and care giving. Along the way, you may come to a better understanding of your own parents and forgive them for mistakes they made. Yet this much is certain: as you learn to cope with the demands of marriage and child rearing, you will discover just how much you have to give and how unselfish you can be. You will find the courage to take on the world for the sake of your children. And you will experience love and tenderness beyond anything you imagined possible.

Children are life's gift to life, inspiring us to provide a healthy, peaceful environment where they can grow up with hope for the future and respect for the dignity of all life. Yet many parents are so busy working to provide for their children that they have to give over to others much of the responsibility for raising them. This Rune urges you to do whatever it takes—make the necessary sacrifices—to be there for your children, especially when they are young.

When we become parents, we are bringing heaven to earth through the soul of a child, and home is where we nourish that connection. By creating an environment where love flourishes and right action is practised, you are establishing a strong foundation for a family that will continue to gather together and appreciate one another for the rest of your lives.

Then again, whether or not you have children of your own, there are always opportunities to nurture: through service in the world, supporting family and friends, caring for or mentoring other people's children. For it is through giving to others that we are truly connected to life.

Finally, this is a Rune of hospitality. Since our willingness to share what we have is a natural expression of who we are, let *Othila* serve as a reminder to always set an extra place at your table and welcome the stranger to your hearth.

> *I am at home within myself wherever I am,*
> *in my family, in my community,*
> *in my country, in the world.*

5   SUPPORT

Uruz

*Since self-change is never coerced—we are always
free to resist—remain mindful that the new life is
always greater than the old.*

> —*The Book of Runes*, Strength

*Wherever you find yourself on the path, be grateful
even for the things you are unable to change, for they
will be your teachers.*

> —*Healing Runes*, Gratitude

In the ancient runic tradition, *Uruz* stood for the wild ox, a beast difficult to domesticate yet prized for its great strength. In the context of meaningful relationships, this Rune represents the generosity of spirit and the readiness to stand by one another that define such a relationship.

At one time or another, even the strongest among us needs support and encouragement. It is important to discover—by asking, paying close attention, listening with an open heart—

how someone you love wishes to be supported and then, to the best of your ability, provide that support in a timely and appropriate manner.

Too often we assume that the needs of another are the same as our own. Acting on such assumptions can cause no end of trouble. Learn to ask and tell each other what you *really* need. After all, when what you long for is warmth and affection, it is disappointing to receive a new set of luggage.

As you become more aware of your sometimes unkind or unconscious responses to someone you care deeply about, and you choose instead to behave in mindful and supportive ways, the quality of your relationship is certain to improve. For this to happen you may be required to identify and abandon some form of behaviour that no longer serves you. Whatever change is called for, know that *only one of you needs to cross the divide for a shift to occur.*

Then there is criticism, which some of us have raised to a fine art. The truth is that criticism is poor fuel and causes any relationship to sputter and run rough. Regardless of the issue, being critical usually means that you are denying another your support. When, instead of looking for the good in a situation, you choose to focus on what your partner is lacking, or on how you would like them to change, you are abusing the heart of relationship itself.

It is possible, however, to give feedback in ways that invite change and growth. For when feedback is offered and received as *helpful information*, both of you are supporting and strengthening the Relationship by enabling one another to do things differently in the future.

Whenever you draw *Uruz*, take a moment to appreciate the things you love about your partner—their strengths, their wisdom, the qualities that attracted you to them in the first place. Acknowledge the ways in which your beloved supports you, makes your life easier, perhaps even possible. One poet spoke of "Love's lovely duty, the well-swept room." In truth, when we sweep for one another, we keep things sweet between us.

Knowing you have someone in your corner who cares about you is always a blessing. When you are supportive—by affirming and encouraging, or simply by being totally present and listening—the Relationship flourishes. Receiving this Rune is an invitation to accept and support those you love without the desire to change them. So say these words of gratitude aloud to each other, and repeat them often:

> *I honor, love and support you*
> *just as you are.*

6

INTIMACY

Perth

Nothing external matters here, except as it shows
you its inner reflection.

—*The Book of Runes*, Initiation

Love is the language in which God speaks. And
when we listen with love, it is the heart that hears.

—*Healing Runes*, Love

In the ancient runic tradition, *Perth* stood for the womb, for something hidden or secret. In the context of meaningful relationships, this translates as the mutual trust that is the binding force of intimacy.

Maybe you are an old hand at intimacy. Then again, perhaps you are just learning to share with a partner your feelings and fears, your secrets and your dreams. Treasure it all, this Rune is saying, for intimacy is a lifelong practice and always worth the effort.

If, however, you are not in an intimate relationship right now, drawing *Perth* is always an opportunity for you to consider how well you are treating *yourself*. And since we can rarely give to another what we do not already possess, it is essential that you learn to treat yourself with the same respect and loving kindness you would give an intimate partner.

Whenever we enter into a loving relationship, we bring with us a reservoir of unmet emotional needs, both from our families of origin and from our previous relationships. Be mindful that this is the case, and be willing to do whatever it takes to heal the wounds of the past. In time, as caring and affection grow between you, fear of intimacy will gradually be replaced by mutual trust.

The challenge in any intimate relationship involves the balancing of our urge for independence with our desire for union. When these strong drives are expressed in positive and healthy ways—in family life, your work in the world, through lovemaking and spiritual practices—you will feel supported both in your going out and your coming in. That is the gift, the Mystery of relationship itself.

As the currents of intimacy flow between you, you will discover that even deeper feelings of tenderness and caring are yours to express. With that discovery will come an appreciation of the many gifts a loving relationship provides—through the sharing of laughter, the sharing of pain, through sharing all that matters most to you. By cherishing and holding each other dear, your awareness of intimacy will expand to include even the ordinary moments of your life together.

Then again, perhaps this Rune has come to you because there are too few expressions of love between you and your partner, or because you no longer feel cherished. Have you stopped to consider your part in what is happening? There are many ways to avoid intimacy, but none to equal withholding. In the long run, our reasons for withholding are irrelevant because the damage caused by a fearful, closed or angry heart can be painfully difficult to repair. So take a moment right now to see your relationship from a larger perspective and remember the love that drew you together in the first place. This Rune encourages you to make the effort to restore the intimacy between you.

Since we all encounter obstacles to intimacy sooner or later, it is essential to remember that, regardless of what is happening in our lives, *how we choose to treat one another is always within our power*. If things have been difficult between you, a tender look or a loving touch may be enough to open the door to intimacy once again. So value intimacy enough to make time for it, for intimacy requires time and a willing heart. Like a powerful tide, intimacy has its own ebb and flow. When it is going out, be patient, be kind, and know that the tide will turn. *Honoring and accepting our partners just as they are, without needing to change them, can be a profound and healing act of love.*

So let your mind be easy about intimacy. The truth is, you were born for it, and true intimacy will mark you as together even when you are separated halfway around the world. That is the grace of relationship. That is heaven on earth.

> *Today I will do something*
> *to delight my beloved's heart.*

7

LIMITATIONS

Nauthiz

*The role of Nauthiz is to identify our shadow, our dark or
repressed side, places where growth has been stunted, resulting
in weaknesses that are often projected onto others.*
—The Book of Runes, Constraint

*Honor yourself for your commitment to the healing journey.
For it is a journey of self-acceptance, self-love and self-care,
a noble journey out of the shadows and into the light.*
—Healing Runes, Shame

In the ancient runic tradition, *Nauthiz* represented the hardships
and sorrows that afflicted humankind. In meaningful relationships,
this Rune is both a call to deal wisely with our limitations and an
opportunity to integrate into our lives the hidden or repressed
aspects of our nature.

Each of us is defined by our strengths and, equally, by our
limitations. While our skills and talents give shape to our
lives, so do the talents and skills we lack. The challenge of this

Rune is to acknowledge our limitations even as we value our strengths, so that we may enjoy healthy relationships with ourselves, our intimate partners, and with all those who are a part of our world.

Then again, who is to say that our limitations are set in stone? A condition that seriously handicapped us at one time or another—a childhood illness, the loss of a parent, a lack of financial means—may no longer pose a problem. So when you find yourself beginning to recite your litany of past failures and defeats, remember that those old stories are guaranteed to leave you feeling powerless, and cast them aside. Rather than dwelling on those things you cannot change, focus instead on what is happening now in your life and give *that* your full attention.

Receiving *Nauthiz* is often a signal that some hidden aspect of who you are is ready to be revealed. We all bring our imperfect selves to every relationship: our fears and addictions, destructive habits that feed on denial, behaviours that we are ashamed of and hope will never come to light. So when we do find the courage to embrace and acknowledge those parts of ourselves that we so often criticize in others, it is compelling evidence of our commitment to change.

Sometimes we hold up mirrors for one another, the better to see our own reflection. Rather than recoil when you don't like what you see, recognize instead the service your partner is performing, and resolve to repair what is ailing, fragmented, or incomplete. For when all is said and done, *the desire and pursuit of wholeness is indeed the way of love.*

When you and your partner commit to sharing with one another the unedited truth of who you are, old wounds and fears are sure to surface so that they may be transformed in the fire of intimate relationship. Once you reclaim the energy it took to withhold or to keep secrets from one another, you will feel an enormous sense of relief. Obstacles that appeared insurmountable will show themselves to be opportunities for growth. Even the most daunting challenges will prove valuable when we recognize them for what they truly are—alchemical moments in which it is possible to turn the lead of our relationships to gold.

When you are troubled by feelings of lack and limitation—lack of a partner, lack of opportunity, the absence of resources or good health—make it your practice to count the blessings that are yours to enjoy. Acknowledge and express gratitude each day for all that is good in your life. For then, regardless of the difficulties you encounter, your decisions will be shaped by a grateful heart.

So welcome the opportunities for growth that *Nauthiz* brings. Few relationships enjoy clear sailing day in, day out. Problems arise. We are disappointed in our expectations. We disappoint and sometimes even betray one another. Yet from accepting who we are, and having the courage to live that truth, comes our strength and the strength of the Relationship itself.

> *I accept and embrace who I am.*
> *I recognize and honor who you are.*
> *Now we are free to change and grow.*

8 RENEWAL

Inguz

*As you resolve and clear away the old, you will
experience a release from tension and uncertainty.*
—*The Book of Runes*, Fertility

*Faith encourages us to believe that we can make a
difference—a difference first in ourselves and then
in the world.*

—*Healing Runes*, Faith

In the ancient runic tradition, this glyph represented the Norse god *Ing* who, while riding in his wagon across the world, brought fertility and plenty to daily life. In the context of meaningful relationships, *Inguz* is the Rune of reconciliation, new beginnings and renewed vows.

Loving relationships are always a valuable resource for personal growth—first for the blessings and gifts we bring to them, and then for the opportunities they inevitably provide for dealing with our unmet needs from the past. When your relationship becomes stuck in emotional gridlock, instead of going your separate ways, are you willing to do the work it takes to realign your hearts? Know that each time the two of you confront and successfully deal with a serious issue, the Relationship itself will be strengthened and renewed.

Renewal is vital to the health and growth of any intimate relationship. So make it your practice to periodically review your life together in order to determine what's working and what's not. If necessary, be willing to reaffirm or even revise your vows. This is a good way to make certain that your agreements are current and shared.

Receiving *Inguz*, ask yourself: "What outcome do I really want in this situation?" Is it to revive and renew your relationship? Or is it more important to you to maintain that you are right even as you sink beneath the waves? You might find it helpful to agree on a time limit for bringing up old offending behaviours—providing, that is, that the old behaviour has indeed changed. Constantly dredging up the past drains life from the present moment, the only moment where the power to change resides.

When, however, the issue is one of betrayal, is renewal even possible? There are so many ways to betray someone you love: by not speaking out or standing firm, by refusing to recognize the truth, by infidelities both great and small. Indeed, there will be situations where neither reason nor logic is of any use, and renewal is only possible when, through forgiveness, you can free yourself from resentment, guilt and blame.

Then again you can love someone, accept who they are, and still choose to leave the relationship. Diverging interests may pull you so far in different directions that there comes a day when you realize you are no longer on the same path. Or one of you persists in unacceptable behaviour long after you have both agreed that the behaviour must change. At such times, perhaps the only way to honor your relationship with yourself is by moving on.

Once you make renewal an integral part of your relationship, it will sustain you through the changing seasons of your life together. When you are committed to supporting each other in this way, the heartbeat of your relationship will be felt in the world.

I am willing to make all things new.

9   RESPECT

Eihwaz

*Patience is the counsel that Eihwaz offers: Nothing
hectic, no acting needy, no lusting after a desired
outcome.*

—*The Book of Runes*, Defence

*This Rune counsels you to open yourself up and
let the light into a part of your life that has been
secret, shut away.*

—*Healing Runes*, Denial

In ancient runic tradition, *Eihwaz* stood for the yew tree and for
the bows crafted from its wood—hard, durable wood possessing
the strength to turn away harm. It is mutual respect that enables
any meaningful relationship to thrive and prosper.

Consider the origin of the word *respect*, derived as it is from
the Latin "to see again." Rather than something you give
or receive, something that is lacking or present in your life,
respect is actually an *ongoing process*, a way of treating yourself

and others, a way of being in the world. It is a process that engages us in the act of returning to any issue again and again in order to see with new eyes, or to see what escaped our eyes before. When you release your need to earn, demand or give respect, *you can embody respect in all that you say and do.*

Whatever the situation confronting you now, be mindful that the ways in which you express yourself—your tone of voice, your body language, your attitude—can affect others more strongly than anything you might actually say in words. So take a moment to ask yourself: Are your conversations friendly or unkind? Do you listen with an open heart and a quiet mind, or are you critical and impatient and do you tend to interrupt? Does forgiveness come easily, or do you withdraw into silent resentment? Although truth is always subject to interpretation, the courtesy and kindness with which you treat one another speaks for itself.

In Zen Buddhist tradition, *all* beliefs are regarded as simply opinions, for it is understood that none of us has the capacity to be truly objective about anything. Learning to treat one another respectfully—by staying present, by listening with and speaking from your heart—builds trust between you, making it easier to resolve conflicts as they arise. And since we are unable to see with God's eyes, it is a good idea not to take our differences of opinion too seriously.

Respect in action is demonstrated by the care we take in appreciating what is important to those we love. Assuming that your partner will automatically feel the way you do indicates a failure of respect. So make it a habit to consult one another about decisions that affect you both, and be willing to discuss an issue until the two of you can agree on the next step to take.

If, however, you find yourselves so attached to your positions that it is impossible to move forward, know that, in addition to your way and your partner's way, there is also *a third way*, a way of listening to the wisdom of the Relationship itself. This open-hearted search for what best serves the Relationship is what respect is all about. When partners learn to approach conflict-resolution and decision-making in this way, the bond between them is invariably strengthened.

Finally, let *Eihwaz* serve as a reminder that two people can disagree and still treat one another respectfully. When we learn to stop seeing each other as the problem, and replace toxic habits like blame and criticism with curiosity and consideration, the need to attack or defend fades away. For where there is mutual respect—regardless of differing desires, opinions, values or beliefs—love will prevail.

The commandment to *Do unto others as you would have others do unto you* is indeed a revolutionary idea when it becomes a natural expression of who you are. Once you align yourself with the power of respect, you will come to recognize it for what it is: a never-ending practice, a practice that demonstrates reverence for life itself.

> *The Divine in me*
> *recognizes and bows*
> *to the Divine in you.*

MUTUAL TRUST

Algiz

*Remain mindful that timely right action and
correct conduct are your only true protection,
and that temperance and courtesy are the sinews
of this Rune's protective powers.*

> —*The Book of Runes*, Protection

*This Rune is a reminder that setting and honoring
appropriate boundaries creates freedom.*

> —*Healing Runes*, Boundaries

In the ancient runic tradition, this glyph stood for an elk's horns or for sedge grass: the horns provided protection and the rustling grass gave notice of approaching danger. In all meaningful relationships, the essential quality of this Rune is still protective, the best protection being mutual trust.

*W*hen a relationship rests on a foundation of mutual trust, there need be no barriers to intimacy. Drawing *Algiz* you are asked to consider: Is the trust between you whole and intact?

Does it flow in both directions? Or are there places where trust has been weakened and, as a result, intimacy is suffering?

Since you can only offer to another what you already possess, self-trust is the foundation for this Rune. So begin by making clear agreements with yourself—and keeping them. Pick something easy, like a daily task you can willingly commit to, then progress to something more difficult, such as changing a particular behaviour or confronting an addiction. As we learn to keep our agreements with ourselves, honoring agreements with others becomes easier and mutual trust grows.

This may be a good time to make an honest inventory of the agreements between you and your partner. Mutual trust dwells in open hearts, hearts that cherish and bless one another. So remember to speak and listen from your heart when you ask, "How well am I keeping my agreements?"

We often betray those we love in small ways, by promises not kept or by words said without thought or feeling. Then there are the difficulties we cause ourselves through *unspoken expectations* that harden into impossible demands, demands that can wreak havoc in any relationship. Learning to bring your unspoken expectations into the light of agreement is essential for the health of mutual trust.

The truth is that sometimes damaged trust can be repaired and sometimes it can't. Receiving *Algiz*, we need to remember what any good gardener knows: if you neglect a plant for too long, it doesn't matter how much you water it. Now is the time, this Rune is saying, to consider the quality of the trust you share.

Finally, remember this: when the love between you is deep, and your intention to respect, support, and cherish one another is strong, there is a good chance that the failures in trust which are bound to occur in any lasting relationship can indeed be healed.

Mutual trust, when present, is always recognizable. Why does it feel so good to be around certain couples? Because there is an ease of communication and a feeling of obvious affection when two people really trust each other. Mutual trust enables us to heal the wounds of the past, enjoy the blessings of partnership in the present, and honor the Mystery of relationship itself. Ultimately, the practice of mutual trust is evidence of our faith in the infinite wisdom of the Divine.

I honor our agreements and cherish
the trust that is growing between us.

ABUNDANCE

II

Fehu

*Enjoy your good fortune and remember to share
it, for the mark of the well-nourished self is the
ability and willingness to nourish others.*
> —*The Book of Runes*, Possessions

*To be honest with oneself is where all healing
begins. For the seeds of the courage to heal can
only grow in honest soil.*
> —*Healing Runes*, Honesty

In the ancient runic tradition, *Fehu* stood for possessions, for cattle, and for the wealth of the community. In the context of meaningful relationships, this Rune speaks of the blessings to be gained through living our lives in gratitude.

This is a Rune of blessings received and blessings bestowed, and recognition of the pleasures to be found in sharing your destiny with another. Receiving *Fehu* is an invitation to take a moment, right now, and count your blessings.

Seduced by dreams of more, better, different, we often take for granted the ordinary joys that make up the weave of our days—the people we care about and those who care about us, honest work, a home-cooked meal, the touch of a loved one's hand. So give thanks for simple pleasures, for they are among the places where earth and heaven meet.

When your heart is filled with gratitude, you will always live life from a place of abundance. For then you can accept any situation in which you find yourself, secure in the knowledge that you possess the resources to handle whatever life may bring, including pain, loss or sorrow. *Wishing nothing to be different than it is at this present moment is to invite abundance into your life.*

There is an old wise proverb that counsels us to make a virtue out of necessity. So take what comes, this Rune is saying, and find the best in it. Since *Fehu* is followed by the Rune of Celebration, remember to celebrate what is sweet in your life at this moment, never forgetting that even with slender means, the sentiments of the heart can be expressed.

At the worst of times it is still within our power to reach out, to love, to show kindness, to share what is ours to share. Hard times honor us by their presence, encouraging us to draw upon our strengths, reminding us of the wealth we call family and friends. *The ability to take joy in each other when life is difficult is a true sign of abundance.*

And what greater abundance is there than our relationship with God? When we learn to live in faith and trust, we abandon our need for control, struggle less and feel our fears subside. As we allow ourselves to be supported and uplifted by Divine

Guidance, abundance takes the form of inner peace and the desire to treat all life with respect and loving kindness.

> *I give thanks and praise*
> *for the abundance*
> *of this moment.*

CELEBRATION

Wunjo

This Rune is a fruit-bearing branch. Now you can rejoice, having been carried across the gap by the will of Heaven.

—*The Book of Runes*, Joy

There is a place inside our being where serenity dwells. Take time each day to nourish yourself with the comfort to be found there.

—*Healing Runes*, Serenity

In the ancient runic tradition, *Wunjo* indicated the presence of joy, a time marked by the absence of suffering and sorrow. In the context of meaningful relationships, this is the Rune of play, delight and shared laughter.

Each time you draw *Wunjo*, regardless of the challenge you may be facing, take it as an invitation to celebrate what is nourishing and pleasing in your life. Find the good and praise it. Celebrate your victories, the hardships you have overcome, a job well done. Celebrate the milestones, the birthdays and anniversaries, exams passed and promotions achieved. Celebrate the family and friends you love and care about and would miss if they were gone from your life. Find the time—make the time— to enjoy and appreciate the blessings that are yours to enjoy.

If you are married or with a partner, let this Rune be a reminder to create daily rituals to celebrate your relationship. Choose something as simple as greeting the new morning together or going for a walk in the evening and sharing the events of your day. The form is unimportant; what matters is the sharing.

It is said that laughter is the best medicine since it releases endorphins, lowers blood pressure and accelerates healing. So take every possible opportunity to laugh together, for when you can find the humor in a situation, almost any challenge becomes easier to manage. Good humor is an ally to keep with you throughout the day, and laughter is a form of rejoicing that gladdens the heart at any hour.

Through all recorded time, dance has been a part of celebration. Have you ever watched lovers while they danced? Few things are more intimate or more beautiful. When did you last take your partner in your arms and dance?

Buddhists recognize a form of love known as *sympathetic joy*, which translates as a feeling of pleasure at the success of others. "Good for you," we say, and we are happy for them. How much more shall this apply to your beloved? There is wisdom in the popular command: "Enjoy!" So celebrate one another in sympathetic joy.

Consider the smiling words of the Hindu mystic Meher Baba:

"Don't worry. Be happy." Since the present is the only time in which to do that, we must be willing to banish fear and resentment from this moment and replace them with serenity and joy. *This is the day that the Lord hath made. Let us rejoice and be glad in it.* To live in gratitude is to live a life of celebration.

Whether you find yourself with a partner or alone, *Wunjo* encourages you to celebrate each day and to embrace the blessings it brings. So have a good time, this Rune is saying, and encourage everyone around you to have a good time. For the one thing you can depend on is that your present situation will change. And when it does, celebrate that!

> *I am filled with gratitude, serenity and joy.*
> *Alone or with another, I celebrate life.*

13 # PERSEVERANCE

Jera

*You have prepared the ground and planted the seed.
Now you must cultivate with care. Know that the
outcome is in the keeping of Providence and
continue to persevere.*

—*The Book of Runes*, Harvest

*Happy is the one whose own heart never lies, who
knows what waiting means, and still can wait.*

—*Healing Runes*, Patience

In the ancient runic tradition, *Jera* stood for a span of time as well as for the fruit of the harvest. In the context of meaningful relationships, this Rune represents our willingness and ability to see things through to completion.

The journey of relationship is exactly that—a journey over time, through many weathers and conditions. Yet there is nothing radical about *Jera*. Here, progress is measured one step, one realization at a time, since without perseverance few meaningful relationships would survive. It is by persevering that we create new habits and attitudes and improve our skills for relating. Once you set your intention to change, you can begin to replace old outmoded behaviour with fresh and creative ways of being together that bring new life to the relationship.

If the present demands of your life leave you feeling exhausted or overwhelmed, this Rune is sent to cheer you on. "Do whatever it takes" is *Jera*'s motto. So if a retreat is necessary to help you find clarity, ask your partner to support you while you take time for renewal. When one of you is running on empty, the other can usually supply the fuel to keep the relationship going. And since every relationship is a work in progress, when hard times find you, remember: this is what you signed on for. This is what you came together to do.

Loyalty and patience are among the essential qualities of this Rune. As are purpose, commitment, determination and courage —the courage to let right action flow through you, the courage to recognize and overcome resistance, to know when to surrender and even the courage to say goodbye.

This Rune can also mark a time of good fortune, a time of patience rewarded, of harvest and thanksgiving. Perseverance leads to the harvest of the self, the harvest that is the beloved returning to its Source. If this is a moment of endings and goodbyes, know that even while you are grieving, it is good to offer prayers of gratitude and praise for the love and beauty you have shared.

So be open to life, be open to adventure, and remember to

look for the humor in times of hardship. This Rune reminds us that we can change when we make change our first priority, and that we always possess the freedom both to persevere and begin again.

> *Patience yields its rewards.*
> *Time brings answers.*
> *To understand is lucky.*

14

INNER PEACE

Kano

*This is the Rune of Opening and renewed clarity,
of dispelling the darkness that has been shrouding
some part of your life.*

—*The Book of Runes*, Opening

*While you may be unable to change your present
situation, what you can do is change your response
to that situation.*

—*Healing Runes*, Acceptance

In the ancient runic tradition, *Kano* stood for a torch, a light to guide travellers on their way. In the context of meaningful relationships, *Kano* is the inner light that guides the compassionate heart.

A peaceful heart and tranquil mind are your rightful inheritance. Let no one tell you differently. So if you are feeling overwhelmed by the pressure of conflicting demands, receiving this Rune is a call to do whatever is necessary to restore harmony and well-being to your life. For then you will be able to observe all that is going on around you through the eyes of inner peace, and you will find the courage and the strength to meet any challenge.

In the stillness of meditation, bring your mind home to this present moment. With practice, you will find ways to shift into the quiet of your observing mind. Whether you are driving in traffic, talking on the phone, preparing a meal, or digging in the garden, when you give your full attention to each moment, everything you do becomes a meditation.

How will you know when inner peace is taking root in your life? Here are some of the signs: Frequent feelings of appreciation and gratitude. Loss of interest in judging others and yourself. A hearty appetite for living in the present moment, released from all fears for the future and unhappy memories from the past. A willingness to allow things to unfold in their own time and in their own way. An abiding awareness of the presence of the Divine in your life.

When you align yourself with the unchanging nature of the Sacred, inner peace is always the result. Living in trust and gratitude—in the sure and certain knowledge that you *can* respond appropriately to whatever life brings—enables you to think clearly and act decisively, even in the hurly burly of tumultuous change. In the timeless wisdom of The Serenity Prayer, you will find the coordinates for inner peace:

> *God grant me the serenity*
> *to accept the things I cannot change,*
> *the courage to change the things I can,*
> *and the wisdom to know the difference.*

Have you ever come across a mountain stream so choked with leaves and branches that the water was barely flowing? And so you set to work to clear away the debris and watched with pleasure as the water broke free and rushed on? When you cease to resist, inner peace can flow freely, refreshing your spirit and easing your heart.

Whenever you receive *Kano*, it is good to relax and let go of the cares of the day. Take a moment, right now, to arrest your mind's habitual craving for distraction. Give up your need to understand or even to make things better. Simply sit in silence, in calm abiding, repeating these words as you follow the in-and-out rhythm of your breath:

> *I breathe out all pain and sorrow*
> *I breathe in love and compassion*
> *I breathe out all tension and fear*
> *I breathe in peace and loving kindness.*

15

PASSION

Teiwaz

*Here you are asked to look within, to delve down
to the foundations of life itself. Only in so doing
can you hope to satisfy the deepest needs of your
nature and tap into your most profound resources.*

—The Book of Runes, Warrior

Courage is faith in action.

—Healing Runes, Courage

In the ancient runic tradition, *Teiwaz* was associated with the Norse god *Tiw*, whose name was invoked to bring victory in battle. In the context of meaningful relationships, this Rune embodies the passion that ignites, energizes and sustains deep intimacy between lovers, as well as between all of us and the Divine.

This Rune is a flare that illuminates the field where lovers meet and passion is the prize. Receiving *Teiwaz* is an invitation to allow yourself intensity of feeling in everything you do. Whether it be your enthusiasm for ideas, the gift of making love, reverence for life or your connection with the Divine—all this is deserving of your passion. Know that it is in our passion for one another that we will recognize God's passion for us.

Few experiences in life can match the irresistible power of new love. While what we call attraction is part of the mystery of intimate relationship, it is usually romance coupled with passion that draws two people together. Love in all its passionate forms allows the heart to open, the soul to soar and the body to experience the bliss of two beings joining and merging. For some of us, that chemistry is happening now.

If your relationship is still in the discovery stage, enjoy the courtship and take your time getting to know each other. Remember to open yourself to receive, since receiving provides your beloved with the pleasure of being the one who gives.

Then again, if the physical passion between you is presently at low ebb, you can still enjoy the intimacy of time spent together with no agenda, simply listening with and speaking from your hearts. Passion evolves and grows as we grow and evolve, nourishing relationship in different ways at different times in our lives. In a mature relationship, when we feel free to reveal to each other all of who we are, that honesty can be a powerful aphrodisiac. Like the phoenix, a passionate relationship endures the fire and can rise again and again from its own ashes, wiser, more compassionate, more deeply loving.

A relationship damaged by jealousy or betrayal can sometimes be healed through passion that is tempered with kindness, forgiveness and understanding. By letting go of your need to be right, and focusing instead on your abiding love for each other, you can find your way back to harmony. It was the

Apostle Peter who said, "Finally, all of you, be of one mind, having compassion one for another." And what is compassion, after all, if not passion's tender face.

Too often, in our need to get ahead in the world, we deny ourselves the healing power of pleasure. We become so caught up in getting and spending that we forgo the joys so readily available to us—walking in nature, playing with a child, making love, delighting in good company—all of which are healing for the spirit. This Rune is a reminder to *let a passionate appreciation of simple pleasures bless all your days.*

So be passionate about your life, passionate about your family and friends, your work, your service in the world. Be passionate in the way you greet each day. Feelings of unworthiness and disappointment, indifference or fatigue, will short-circuit passion, weaken the immune system, and diminish your capacity for healing. Therefore, be open to passion in all its diverse forms, for passion can be a staunch ally. Come to know yourself, this Rune is saying, as a person committed to living a passionate life.

Finally, *Teiwaz* serves to remind us that there is an unbreakable connection between passion, our love for one another, our love of God, and God's love for us. We are all warriors of the Spirit and in our passion is both the fire and the movement of love.

I choose to live a passionate life.

131

16 RIGHT ACTION

Berkana

You may be required to cultivate the soil once again,
yet through correct preparation, growth is assured.
                                        —*The Book of Runes*, Growth

It is through prayer that we practise the presence of
God in our lives.

                                        —*Healing Runes*, Prayer

In the ancient runic tradition, *Berkana* symbolized the awakening of nature in spring, a time of fertility, fruitfulness and the birth of new life. In the context of meaningful relationships, this Rune stands for the practice of right action in all our thoughts, words and deeds.

What does it mean to practise right action? Simply put, even when no one is watching, and no one will ever find out, you still choose to do what you believe in your heart is right. Ultimately, right action is the grace through which we align our lives with the will of the Divine. *I will to will Thy will* is a powerful affirmation for right action.

Consider the law of cause and effect which affirms that everything you do, each action taken or not taken, has consequences, and that those consequences actually shape your future. You know you are practising right action when what you think, feel, and say are in accord with what you do.

Receiving *Berkana*, take a moment to consider where right action is called for in your relationship. If something is causing you pain, begin by communicating your concerns to your partner without blaming them or making them wrong. Even when passions and tempers are running high, right action requires that you express your feelings honestly, without attacking, and with the intention of resolving the problem. And since we tend to change exceedingly slowly, be patient with one another, bearing in mind the advice of tailors and carpenters to "measure twice, cut once."

Is there some issue in your life that calls for forgiveness? There are times when forgiveness is crucial to the health of a relationship, when in fact it is the only form right action can take. For with true forgiveness comes the ability to open your heart, leave the past behind, and get on with your life.

A relationship is a living system that thrives upon right action. However, when two people have strong yet conflicting desires, it can be helpful to take a step back and do something unusual: *Ask the Relationship itself what it needs*. Put yourself in the place of your Relationship and let it speak through you to communicate its needs, its dreams. As you and your partner become familiar with this kind of listening, you will begin to appreciate the wisdom of the "Third," the wise voice of the Relationship itself.

Since right action guides every aspect of a loving relationship, after receiving *Berkana*, you may want to draw a second Rune. Doing so can help you to identify the form right action might take, whether it be support, respect, mutual trust or even celebration.

Finally, this Rune is a reminder that when we treat relationship as sacred, all of life becomes sacred. So listen to your heart and let right action flow through you, for the fruit of right action is a peaceful spirit.

> *Let right action guide me*
> *in everything I think, say and do*

17   LETTING GO

Ehwaz

Ehwaz is a Rune of transit and transition, of new dwelling places, new attitudes or new life. Let it be said this way: As I cultivate my own nature all else follows.
　　　　　　　　　　　　　　—The Book of Runes, Movement

A life in transition draws upon forgiveness in order to make peace with the past. Who is it that calls out to you for forgiveness? To whom do you call out?
　　　　　　　　　　　　　　—Healing Runes, Forgiveness

In the ancient runic tradition, *Ehwaz* stood for the horse as well as for the sun's journey across the sky. The horse was treasured for its strength and the sun was venerated as the source of life and fruitfulness. In the context of meaningful relationships, this Rune represents the process of releasing the old so that you can welcome and appreciate the new.

I t has been said that a perfect statue lies hidden within the stone and that the sculptor works to set it free, chipping away patiently, stroke by measured stroke. The same could be said of loving relationships, for as we chip away our illusions and projections, our unrealistic expectations and our fears, the true nature of the relationship is revealed.

Often this calls for breaking with habits that no longer serve us, ridding ourselves of excess baggage we brought with us into the relationship. To do so requires strength, determination, and sometimes the willingness to ask for help. Your readiness to reach out will support you in finding the courage to release the old, the courage to change those things you can change, the courage to live your life in trust.

During times of major transition and change, we must free ourselves from the past in order to welcome what is to come. You have been a parent for half your life and overnight the children are gone. The company where you worked for twenty years has been sold and your job no longer exists. You have just been diagnosed with a serious illness and your lifestyle must change radically. So what do you do now?

Often it helps to envision what you want to create in order to give new direction to your life. Yet if you are too focused on a specific outcome, you may fail to take advantage of an opportunity that is right before your eyes. Stay present, this Rune is saying. And remember, even when you feel you have no control over what is happening in your life, how you choose to respond—your attitude—is always up to you. Know with absolute certainty that you are free to wake up any morning and begin again.

Releasing our attachment to the unhappy stories of our past—the love we never received from our parents, the betrayals, the failures and unrealized dreams—frees us to fully embrace this present moment, to be here now, alive, refreshed, filled with gratitude and open to new possibilities. Learning to see the past with new eyes, acknowledging that you are not that person anymore, is a rewarding approach to self-change.

For some of us, receiving this Rune may call for a close examination of an important relationship. Perhaps the time has come to move on—alone, wiser, stronger than you were before. If that is the case, give thanks for the gifts this relationship has brought you, and release it, bearing in mind that when it comes to letting go, acceptance and forgiveness are often the keys.

Receiving *Ehwaz*, it is good to consider the end of our own allotted time and to begin preparing for that moment. Perhaps our death is the letting go for which all the others are merely rehearsals. Yet one thing is certain: when you do surrender, a shift occurs. Letting go is a significant form of self-mastery, so become a black belt in the art of letting go.

> *Letting go of the past,*
> *I am free to wake up each morning*
> *and begin again.*

18

CHANGE

Laguz

The attributes of this Rune are water, fluidity, the ebb and flow of emotions, careers, and relationships.
—*The Book of Runes*, Flow

Humor is healing's handmaiden.
—*Healing Runes*, Humor

In the ancient runic tradition, *Laguz* stood for water, the source of fertility, the essence of life. In the realm of meaningful relationships, this Rune supports our ability to adapt well in times of transition and change.

A*ll is flux, nothing remains the same, nothing endures but change*. So wrote the Greek philosopher Heraclitis 2,500 years ago. Today this Rune speaks to our willingness and ability to accept change gracefully—to be flexible, to modify habitual behaviours and to grow.

Openness to change is essential to the yoga of relationship. Receiving *Laguz*, consider what changes are being asked of you now in order for your relationship to prosper. Is there a need for greater honesty between you? Greater awareness of when you are being judgmental or resisting the obvious need to adapt? A call for more time spent together or apart?

The health of any relationship depends upon your willingness to embrace change in ways that accommodate your own growth, your partner's well-being, and the health of the Relationship itself. The good news is that only one of you must acknowledge the need for change in order for the process to begin.

When you are faced with the inevitability of change, sometimes it helps to *simply let go into the stillness of not knowing*. Releasing your hold on the comfortable, the familiar, can be a blessing. Clinging to the past, fear of the future, pride, the need to control, the mistaken idea that everything would be fine if only your partner would do things differently—these are among the greatest obstacles to change. So make change your ally and allow its energy to lift you up and move you forward.

"Act as if and you will become"is a powerful affirmation both for self-change and for healing. The prayers that accompany it are prayers of thanksgiving—offering thanks in advance for what, at this moment, exists only in our minds and hearts. So rather than praying to God to heal your relationship, visualize it instead as already healthy and whole, and give thanks for that.

The plow of change invariably cuts across the furrows of our settled lives. When radical change is thrust upon us, we always have a choice: we can resist, or we can choose to adapt to the new conditions in which we find ourselves. Even when you are grieving for the end of a relationship or the death of a loved one, it is comforting to remember that grief too has its half life, and that passing time will ease the intensity of your suffering.

One encouraging truth about the turbulent times in which we live is this: *Nobody really knows what to do next.* And that, curiously enough, makes all of us more equal than we have ever been before. So be kind to everyone you meet along the way, for you never know from what direction the answers will come.

Many of the qualities associated with water are, likewise, attributes of change. Change rushes, it cleanses, it sweeps away debris. If wave after wave of change has left you feeling anxious, frustrated and overwhelmed, take a moment to appreciate how far you have come in order to reach this place. Accept that you will always be changing, always arriving, always moving on.

So become a lover of change, for then, even when what you are facing carries a high degree of strangeness and discomfort, you can welcome it as a divine tide flowing through your life.

> *Knowing that what is mine will come to me,*
> *I release the old and give thanks for the blessings*
> *of my life. I am ready and willing to embrace change.*

19

CHALLENGES

Hagalaz

What you regard as detours, inconveniences,
disruptions, blockages, and even failures and deaths,
will actually be rerouting opportunities, with union
and reunion as the only abiding destinations.

—*The Book of Runes*, Disruption

You must give up the old and be willing to wait
patiently for the new to be revealed to you in its
proper time.

—*Healing Runes*, Anger

In the ancient runic tradition, *Hagalaz* stood for hail and sleet, natural forces that caused damage to crops and made life more difficult for humankind. In the context of meaningful relationships, this Rune indicates the presence of demanding situations that call for us to respond with dignity, courage and an open heart.

W̶e live in a world filled with challenges—conditions and situations that are often beyond our ability to control or even influence. Plans fall apart, life disappoints us, we disappoint one another. When such is the case, regardless of the seriousness of the challenge you are facing, there is one key element over which you do have control: *How you choose to respond is always up to you.*

In every caring relationship, there will come times when you lose touch with your abiding love for each other. If that is the case now, begin by recognizing your role in what is happening and take responsibility for it. Sometimes talking helps. Yet when tempers flare and you find yourself saying things that are better left unsaid, it often helps to take a break and come together again after both of you have recovered your self-control and, hopefully, your sense of humor. For then you can approach any situation, however difficult, in the way of true partners—by speaking from your hearts and listening with your hearts.

Seen in a certain light, everything is a challenge. Yet what if the obstacle you are presently facing is greater than your strength to meet it? There will be times when the benefits gained from learning how to handle yourself well in failure and defeat can take the form of surprising new skills, broader vision and greater peace of mind. Know that both hardship and success are master teachers, that even sorrow can be a worthy companion, and that our mistakes often contain valuable information about how to do things differently next time.

And then there are rewarding challenges, like becoming a parent, moving to a new job in a new town, or taking another chance on love. *Hagalaz* encourages you to welcome change in its every form, do what is called for to the best of your ability, then release the outcome and place it in the hands of Divine Providence.

Count it a blessing when you have a loving partner to face life's challenges with you. However, if you are not in an intimate relationship at present, look around you and you will discover that there *are* people in your life who love and support you, people who will be there for you when you ask.

In Chinese, the word for crisis is made up of two characters, one representing "danger" and the other "opportunity." This may well be the moment to convert what feels like a danger into an opportunity. So welcome this challenge as your teacher and friend.

> *How I choose to respond to any challenge*
> *is always up to me. This is my strength.*

20

HARMONY

Raido

*You are concerned here with nothing less than
unobstructed perfect union. Heaven above you and
Earth below you unite within you to support you
on your way.*

—*The Book of Runes*, Journey

*Surrender is the highest form of conscious contact
with the Divine.*

—*Healing Runes*, Surrender

In the ancient runic tradition, this glyph stood for life's journey as well as the journey of the soul after death. *Raido* was valued as a talisman to ensure a successful passage. In the context of meaningful relationships, this Rune calls for us to learn to accept and appreciate our differences.

E very harmonious relationship makes a music all its own, separate melodic themes that will, with patience and perseverance, blend smoothly in two-part harmony. There is much pleasure to be found in talking intimately, making plans, dreaming and laughing together; pleasure in being quiet or saying out loud, "I'm glad you're in my life." Whenever two people share common values, experiences, and interests, even hardship and defeat can be handled with a peaceful heart.

Harmony must first come from within. After all, how can you be in harmony with another when you are in conflict with yourself? If such is the case, acknowledge that you are feeling troubled or anxious. Then take a deep breath, let go of everything—your painful memories of the past, your worries for the future, all your expectations—and relax into the present moment, the only place where harmony is to be found.

If harmony is lacking in your relationship right now, *Raido* urges you to create a safe space where the two of you can sit together and discuss the issues that are troubling you. Start by putting yourself in your partner's place in order to understand how their needs may differ from your own. Ask each other what must change in order to restore balance between you. Then seek to find a new way of being together that you can both embrace.

Few things cause more mischief in a relationship than unrealistic expectations. Assumptions such as: "My partner will always be interested in what interests me... He will want to make love whenever I do... She will always be there for me, no matter what..." To the extent that you hold on to such expectations, you are bound to be disappointed. On the other hand, as you shed your illusions about your partner, you free yourself to accept and love them exactly as they are, no exceptions, no exclusions. That is unconditional love in action.

When your desire for harmony is strong, acceptance and

reconciliation require less effort, and the common sense of philosopher William James' words is easy to appreciate: "The art of being wise is the art of knowing what to overlook." To maintain a harmonious relationship, both of you must become peacemakers, for the power of peaceful persuasion is unsurpassed among skilful means.

It can be helpful to think of your relationship as an extended journey. So begin by making an inventory of your attachments, then ask yourself what is best left behind—old attitudes, old habits, sometimes even old friends—in order for the journey to be successful.

Then, too, when you both acknowledge that intimate relationship is also a *spiritual* journey, you can practise opening yourselves consciously to Spirit, to the will of God, by praying or meditating together, sharing a love for nature, doing service in the world and by being firmly committed to living together in harmony.

Here are the words from a Hawaiian song to support you on your way:

> *From you I receive*
> *To you I give.*
> *Together we share*
> *From this we live.*

21

COMPROMISE

Thurisaz

*Impulses must be tempered by thought for correct
procedure. Be still, collect yourself, and wait on the
Will of Heaven.*

—*The Book of Runes*, Gateway

*Wisdom teaches the mind to understand and learn
through love.*

—*Healing Runes*, Wisdom

In the ancient runic tradition, *Thurisaz* was associated with the
Norse god Thor, the benevolent protector of his people. In the
province of meaningful relationships, this Rune guides us to be
compassionate and caring with each other through our ability
and willingness to compromise.

S ince no two people are ever perfectly matched in their needs
and preferences, there will come times when you are unable
to reach an agreement and yet a decision is necessary.
Compromise supports movement, while the ability to put

yourself in your partner's place is a way of saying, "I recognize that this is important to you." Drawing *Thurisaz* ask yourself: Are you open to your partner's request for change? Is your partner open to yours? There will be situations where you recognize that choosing to honor your partner's needs over your own is, indeed, the right thing to do. Readiness to compromise is strong evidence of your commitment to one another and to the well-being of the Relationship.

If the present challenge is simply to get off "stuck," do whatever it takes to disengage, bearing in mind that sometimes the wisest action is to take no action at all. When you find yourself incapable of compromise, it can be helpful to put your issue on hold, since what seems impossible today may prove effortless tomorrow.

Many of us have lived our lives believing that in order to compromise we must give something up. Yet there is another approach, one that *welcomes compromise as an exploration of new possibilities*. When you are open to finding solutions that benefit you, your partner, and the Relationship itself, then each successful compromise becomes a course adjustment that allows your sails to catch the wind once again.

While the willingness to compromise is essential to the health of every relationship, you both harm yourself and sabotage the Relationship if you constantly put your partner's needs and concerns ahead of your own. When you find that you are the one who invariably does the accommodating, you have crossed the line from meaningful compromise to inappropriate self-sacrifice.

There may be times, however, when you simply cannot compromise. Some things are not negotiable and it is not appropriate to back down or give in. If your emotional or physical health is at risk, or if your partner refuses to take seriously your concern over core issues—issues of abuse, morality, integrity—it may be time to pack your bags and leave.

Some of us are old hands at compromise. Yet, with practice, even a novice will come to appreciate compromise for its healing and restorative value. "I have no cherished outcomes" is a powerful affirmation that supports our willingness and ability to embrace change.

Finally, there are people who say, "Never compromise your beliefs." Yet if our beliefs hold us in thrall or hold us apart, how shall we reason together? How can peace prevail? While our ultimate responsibility is to be true to ourselves, those who become skilled in the art of compromise while retaining their individuality, make harmonious companions on the journey of loving relationship.

> *As surely as your way is distinct*
> *from my way, there is in all matters*
> *also a third way. To find it, let us pass*
> *together through the gates of compromise.*

22

PURPOSE

Dagaz

Drawing Dagaz *often signals a major shift or*
breakthrough in the process of self-change. Rely,
therefore, on radical trust, even though the moment
may call for you to leap empty-handed into the void.
　　　　　　　—The Book of Runes, Breakthrough

Rather than collapse yourself into thoughts of
the future, stay in the present, for considerable
hard work is involved in a time of healing and
transformation.

　　　　　　　　　　　　—Healing Runes, Hope

In the ancient runic tradition, this Rune symbolized the power of daylight to foster prosperity and security in a world of darkness. In the context of our meaningful relationships, *Dagaz* represents the light of shared purpose that gives deeper meaning to our lives.

Drawing *Dagaz* is a reminder that we fulfill our purpose and manifest our destiny with each step we take in the present.

So it is good to remember the old saying, "A job worth doing is worth doing well." For when you commit to giving your best in all that you do, your life will unfold in satisfying and often surprising ways.

With this Rune come interesting questions. What is the purpose of this relationship? Is it a friendship, a partnership, a lifetime commitment? Can we accomplish together what neither of us could accomplish alone? How can we be of service to each other, to our families, our friends, and to the world? Keeping the lines of communication between you open and honest will help to define and put into practice the guiding principles for your life together.

Partners who remain together for many years often commit to some goal or undertaking that brings a shared focus to their relationship. Raising and caring for children is a purpose that lasts a lifetime. Going into business together, creating a home, committing to a spiritual practice—all of these can help to strengthen and deepen our appreciation and love for one another. And when you commit to supporting each other's dreams, your relationship will become a partnership that nourishes your creativity as well as your spirit.

In Proverbs it is written: "Where there is no vision, the people perish." Vision sharpens the wits of purpose, aids us in setting priorities, fortifies our agreements, and guides us into service—service to one another, to this earth and, through it all, service to the Divine. Purpose, then, is vision in action.

When your life is illuminated by the clear light of purpose, you will meet challenges with greater patience and handle disappointments with determination and good will. Experiences that once felt like failures or defeats will, with time, reveal themselves as necessary and sufficient for your growth. Every crisis you meet and manage will offer new insights and prepare you to appreciate more fully the pleasures and rewards that true purpose brings.

If, however, you are feeling empty and uninspired, the ground rules are simple: stay present. Focus on something that brings you satisfaction. Undertake tasks you *know* you can handle, until you feel your sense of purpose being rekindled and renewed.

In such challenging times as these, there is much to be gained from learning to live with uncertainty. So take a risk and open yourself to the excitement of the unknown. Doing so, you will discover a rare kind of peace and the freedom that comes from living in trust.

Ultimately, it is the purpose of relationship to serve as a vehicle for spiritual awakening. And while needs change and visions evolve, a life informed by purpose supports a relationship capable of growth and transformation.

May the power of purpose and clear intention
provide us with healing and delight
on the journey of relationship.

23

REFLECTION

Isa

What has been full must empty, what has increased
must decrease. This is the way of heaven and earth.
To surrender is to display courage and wisdom.
                              —*The Book of Runes*, Standstill

This Rune is a gentle reminder to acknowledge the
power of change.

                              —*Healing Runes*, Fear

In the ancient runic tradition, *Isa* stood for those times when life came to a standstill, when the earth was frozen and the season of waiting was upon the people. In the context of meaningful relationships, this Rune serves as a reminder that receptivity and the ability to wait are essential aspects of reflection.

Receiving this Rune is a call for stillness and reflection. So give yourself time to consider: How am I living my life? What are my priorities? What are my expectations? If you are convinced that your happiness depends on persuading your partner to change in some way, let *Isa* serve as a reminder that the only person you can change is yourself. So whatever challenge you may be facing now, choose stillness over action. Choose reflection.

If the energy between you feels blocked or frozen, instead of doubting yourself or your partner, allow for the periodic maintenance and repair that every relationship requires. Set yourself winter tasks. Examine old ways of behaving that put a strain on the Relationship. It could be something as obvious as always needing to be right, or insisting on having the last word. And remember this: habits that may have saved your life as a child—outbursts of rage, withdrawing, never letting anyone know what you were truly feeling—are bound to sabotage a mature relationship.

Sometimes this Rune introduces the period of gestation that precedes a birth, that mysterious time in nature when nothing stirs and yet everything is preparing for new life. Yet this much we know: when the old way has come to an end and the new has yet to reveal itself, the challenge is to make peace with not knowing. So take refuge in prayer and meditation. Be ready to reinvent yourself, to reinvent your relationship. At such times reflection is your ally.

All relationships have their fallow periods, times when you realize that what once served you well is no longer working and that you both want something more. At such a time, this Rune's counsel is to reach out for help. If that feels appropriate, find a wise friend or a therapist, someone who has successfully guided others through their rough patches. Sound guidance, combined with a willingness to look within can provide the energy to restart a stalled relationship.

When the communication between you is less than loving, taking a break from one another can help you to regain your perspective. In fact, most couples benefit by taking time apart— time for reflection and retreat or even time with close friends or family—after which you may well greet each other with renewed appreciation and love.

Then, too, any intimate relationship is blessed by the creation of sacred space—a day, or even a few hours spent together each week—away from the phone and the children, away from life's never-ending round of activities and responsibilities. A special time set aside for the benefit of the Relationship itself.

And through it all, remember to practise patience, first with yourself, then with your partner. To be patient is to be loving, since the love of which we speak is always patient.

There are cycles to every enduring relationship. At any given moment we are either moving closer together or further apart. Failure to recognize and honor these natural rhythms can lead to the breakdown of an otherwise durable and desirable union. When reflection is called for, it is comforting to remember that if you are receptive and patient, gentle with your partner and with yourself, love will prevail.

In stillness and reflection
I come to know the patience that is love.

24 HEALING

Sowelu

A Rune of great power, Sowelu marks a time for regeneration right down to the cellular level.
                              —*The Book of Runes*, Wholeness

It has been said that when we have compassion for one another, we shall be of one mind.
                              —*Healing Runes*, Compassion

In the ancient runic tradition, *Sowelu* stood for the power of the sun to provide warmth and health, and to make the earth fruitful. In the context of meaningful relationships, this translates as the energy for healing and for making whole that which is ailing, fragmented or incomplete.

Loving relationships, when they are healthy, possess a powerful capacity to heal. If your relationship is presently in need of healing, begin by being honest with one another about any unresolved issues you may have. Is there some health problem you ought to discuss? A dispute about money that needs to be resolved? A betrayal you are afraid to confront? Often receiving *Sowelu* is a plea for amnesty.

This Rune brings with it the promise that *you can heal emotional wounds of the past from where you find yourself in the present*. Although it is impossible to alter past events, when you realize that your "old stories" are barriers to healing, you can shift the way you relate to those events and that shift permits healing in the present.

We are speaking here of the blessings of acceptance and forgiveness. The relief that comes from being forgiven by another often makes it possible for us to forgive ourselves for mistakes we have made, to let go of guilt, and resolve to behave differently in the future. Each time you find it in your heart to forgive, the release of old hurt, resentment, anger and regret is profoundly healing.

Forgiveness can take years or it can be accomplished in an instant. So be patient with yourself, be kind. For when the shift finally does occur, the pain in your heart will subside. However, when forgiveness is inconceivable, know that it is still possible to make peace with what happened, close the door on the relationship, and get on with your life.

For many of us, receiving the Rune of Healing is a call to take better care of ourselves. If you have made a commitment to your emotional or spiritual well-being, drawing this Rune is a reminder to honor that commitment. If you are concerned about some aspect of your physical health, it is time to confront your fears and take action.

Perhaps *Sowelu* has come to you at a challenging moment in your life. An important relationship is ending. Someone you love is ill or dying. At such times, it is good to remember that *even when no cure is possible, healing can still take place.* Reconciliation, forgiveness, acceptance and prayer all play their parts, as do gratitude for the gifts the Relationship has brought you, and a renewed recognition of just how precious life is.

Look to be of service this day, since healing is also found in service—service to your beloved, to your family, to the various communities of which you are a part, and through it all, service to the Divine. Let your relationships be channels for service, expressions of love's generous nature, and a force for healing in the world.

Since the healing power of prayer is profound, if you are in need, be willing to ask others for their prayers. When you are the recipient of focused prayer, it both lifts you up and touches all those who are praying for you. And when you pray for another, the energy of prayer moving through you is also healing you. So live your life in the certain knowledge that you will be healed, and always give thanks in advance for the healing you require.

Finally, remember this: each time we pray for healing, we are united with people all around the world who, in that same moment, are offering up their prayers. And so we pray together now:

> *Wherever it is needed, let there be healing.*
> *Heal our bodies, our minds, our hearts and our spirits.*
> *Heal us, we pray, and make us whole.*

THE MYSTERY

The Blank Rune

*Willingness and permitting are what this Rune
requires, for how can you exercise control over
what has not yet taken form?*
> —*The Book of Runes*, Unknowable

*Divine love nurtures us, comforts us, inspires
and teaches us, and, at the end, calls us home.*
> —*Healing Runes*, The Divine

In the ancient runic tradition, there was no Blank Rune. This twenty-fifth stone is a contemporary innovation that embodies faith, prayer, the working of the Divine in our lives and the mystery of Relationship itself.

The Blank Rune represents true north on the compass of meaningful relationship. Like mariners who navigate by winds and currents to reach their destination, charting your course by the Mystery makes sacred the journey itself. Once you have embarked on the voyage, you will come to realize that union without awareness of the presence of the Sacred is a poor thing. This Rune is the ground for more perfect union, union with an intimate partner, union with the Divine.

Every stage of relationship brings its blessings. The excitement and passion of the unknown when you first discover your love for one another can mature over time into a deep appreciation, a seamless energetic flow that nourishes both you and those around you. Often the challenge in a marriage or a long-term relationship is to learn to release that which once served you well in order to appreciate and value what is now coming to be. For when we give up our cravings for more, better, different, we open ourselves to the creative currents of change. We enter into the Mystery and the Mystery enters into us.

In time you will come to experience your relationship as more powerful than anything either of you could have conceived alone. So cherish, nurture and be grateful for one another. And during those painful moments when you have lost touch with the love that first brought you together, remember this: *Love is your abiding destiny and your natural condition.* For it is through loving one another that we experience intimacy with the Divine.

Intimacy wears a coat of many colours. Tenderness and laughter, loyalty, openness to change, passion and inner peace, the willingness to forgive—we see flashes of it everywhere. Especially in our relationship with children, for they are the very heart of the Mystery. They are its seeds, its fruit and our best reason for celebration. When we are caring for the children, we are always in the presence of the Mystery.

Finally, this Rune is a reminder that to live your life in the awareness of God's presence, you must open yourself to receive the gifts of Spirit. Therefore, abandon your need for control, be willing to live in trust and, even in your darkest hours, hold fast the knowledge that the good will come to you. Waste not a moment, this Rune is saying, to embrace the Mystery as it is unfolding in your life now.

> *Love is my abiding destiny*
> *and my natural condition.*

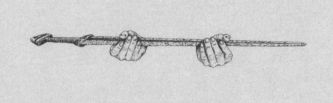

ENVOI

Wanting for nothing, how shall I be dismayed?

Grieving for no thing lost or unattained,

Why would I choke on the sharp bones of regret?

I am a guest in this house: Thoughtful of my manners,

Mindful of my privileges, and so filled with gratitude

That when I pray, my prayers turn to praise upon my lips.

Were I to die just as I am, surrounded so with beauty,

My soul, returning to its source, opened wide

And revealing the map of my journey,

Would show forth, undiminished, beauty only, only beauty.

And so, Beloved, I have written this poem for you.

—R.B.

APPRECIATION

Dear Bones,
It was terrible,
It was wonderful.
And love prevailed.
Bless you for four & a half years
of heartfelt effort,
for helping me pare down
95 categories to 24,
and for your loving words
which are strewn like forget-me-nots
among the fields of my words.
Thanks to you, I am more awake.

For David,
whose patience, wisdom, love and support in all ways
made it possible to complete this work.

For the many friends and family members
whose comments, suggestions
and shared life experiences so enriched the mix.

WE BLESS AND THANK YOU.

PRONUNCIATION GUIDE

	GERMANIC		SOUND VALUE OF THE GERMANIC AS IN MODERN ENGLISH
1.	*Mannaz*	man-naz	*a* as in father
2.	*Gebo*	gay-bo	*e* as in play, *o* as in go
3.	*Ansuz*	an-sooz	*a* as in father, *u* as in ooze
4.	*Othila*	o-the-la	*o* as in go, *th* as in thin, *i* as in meet, *a* as in father
5.	*Uruz*	oo-rooz	*u* as in ooze
6.	*Perth*	perth	*e* as in berth
7.	*Nauthiz*	now-thiz	*au* as in now, *th* as in thin, *i* as in is
8.	*Inguz*	ing-gooz	*ing* as in spring, *u* as in ooze
9.	*Eihwaz*	a-waz	*ei* as in play, *a* as in father
10.	*Algiz*	al-gez	*a* as in father, *g* as in gem, *i* as in meet
11.	*Fehu*	fa-hew	*e* as in play, *u* as in hew
12.	*Wunjo*	woon-jo	*u* as in wound, *j* as in joy, *o* as in go
13.	*Jera*	jer-a	*j* as in join, *e* as in yes, *a* as in father
14.	*Kano*	ka-no	*a* as in father, *o* as in go
15.	*Teiwaz*	ta-waz	*ei* as in play, *a* as in father
16.	*Berkana*	ber-ka-na	*e* as in berry, *a* as in father
17.	*Ehwaz*	eh-waz	*eh* as in yes, *a* as in father
18.	*Laguz*	la-gooz	*a* as in father, *u* as in ooze
19.	*Hagalaz*	ha-ga-laz	*a* as in father, *g* as in give
20.	*Raido*	ri-tho	*ai* as in ride, *d* as in though, *o* as in go
21.	*Thurisaz*	thu-ri-saz	*th* as in thin, *u* as in pull, *i* as in easy, *a* as in father
22.	*Dagaz*	tha-gaz	*d* as in that, *a* as in father
23.	*Isa*	e-sa	*i* as in easy, *a* as in father
24.	*Sowelu*	so-wa-loo	*o* as in go, *e* as in way, *u* as in ooze

ABOUT THE AUTHORS

RALPH BLUM

Ralph received his degree in Russian Studies from Harvard University. Following two years in Italy as a Fulbright Scholar, he returned to Harvard where he did graduate work in anthropology on grants from The National Science Foundation and the Ford Foundation. Encountering the Runes while doing research in England, he subsequently explored their origins and reinterpreted their meanings in terms appropriate for our times.

He is the author of *The Book of Runes*, *RunePlay*, *RuneCards* and *Little Book of Runic Wisdom* and co-author of *Healing Runes* (with Susan Loughan) and *The Serenity Runes* (with Susan Loughan and Bronwyn Jones). *Relationship Runes: A Compass for the Heart* is the seventh title in this oracular series. Ralph Blum has been working with the Runes as a tool for self-counselling since 1979.

He is married to Jeanne Elizabeth Blum, author of *Woman Heal Thyself* and *The Tao of Body Piercing*.

BRONWYN JONES

Bronwyn Jones is the editor of *The Book of Runes*, *RunePlay*, *RuneCards* and *Little Book of Runic Wisdom* and co-author of *The Serenity Runes* and *Relationship Runes: A Compass for the Heart*. She makes her home with her beloved partner, David, in the San Jacinto mountain village of Idyllwild, California, and has been writing and teaching about the Runes since 1981.

Welcome to The RuneWorks

For many people, getting acquainted with the Runes has been an exciting adventure in self-discovery. We would be most interested to hear of your experiences with the Oracle.

If you wish to be placed on our mailing list, please write to us at the address below. Although there are no events scheduled for now, if you are interested in setting up a Rune workshop or lecture on *Relationship Runes: A Compass for the Heart*, we would be happy to work with you to make this possible.

We look forward to hearing from you.

Gud blessi thig.

Bronwyn and Ralph

The RuneWorks

P.O. Box 1193
Idyllwild, CA 92549
Phone: 909-659-5934
Bronwyn's e-mail: theruneworks@verizon.net
Ralph's e-mail: blumblum@earthlink.net

		Book of Runes	Healing Runes	Relationship Runes	Germanic Name
1	ᛗ	The Self	Innocence	Loving Kindness	*Mannaz*
2	ᚷ	Partnership	Trust	Commitment	*Gebo*
3	ᚨ	Signals	Guilt	Communication	*Ansuz*
4	ᛟ	Separation	Grief	Home & Family	*Othila*
5	ᚢ	Strength	Gratitude	Support	*Uruz*
6	ᛈ	Initiation	Love	Intimacy	*Perth*
7	ᚾ	Constraint	Shame	Limitations	*Nauthiz*
8	ᛜ	Fertility	Faith	Renewal	*Inguz*
9	ᛇ	Defence	Denial	Respect	*Eihwaz*
10	ᛉ	Protection	Boundaries	Mutual Trust	*Algiz*
11	ᚠ	Possessions	Honesty	Abundance	*Fehu*
12	ᚹ	Joy	Serenity	Celebration	*Wunjo*
13	ᛃ	Harvest	Patience	Perseverance	*Jera*
14	ᚲ	Opening	Acceptance	Inner Peace	*Kano*
15	ᛏ	Warrior	Courage	Passion	*Teiwaz*
16	ᛒ	Growth	Prayer	Right Action	*Berkana*
17	ᛖ	Movement	Forgiveness	Letting Go	*Ehwaz*
18	ᛚ	Flow	Humor	Change	*Laguz*
19	ᚺ	Disruption	Anger	Challenges	*Hagalaz*
20	ᚱ	Journey	Surrender	Harmony	*Raido*
21	ᚦ	Gateway	Wisdom	Compromise	*Thurisaz*
22	ᛞ	Breakthrough	Hope	Purpose	*Dagaz*
23	ᛁ	Standstill	Fear	Reflection	*Isa*
24	ᛋ	Wholeness	Compassion	Healing	*Sowelu*
25	☐	Unknowable	The Divine	The Mystery	*Blank Rune*